Blended Learning

Blended Learning

Across the Disciplines, Across the Academy

Edited by Francine S. Glazer

Foreword by James Rhem

Published in Association with the National Teaching and Learning Forum

STERLING, VIRGINIA

Sty/us

COPYRIGHT © 2012 BY
STYLUS PUBLISHING, LLC.

Published by Stylus Publishing, LLC.
22883 Quicksilver Drive
Sterling, Virginia 20166-2102

Library of Congress Cataloging-in-Publication Data
Blended learning : across the disciplines, across the academy / edited by Francine S. Glazer ; foreword by James Rhem.
    p. cm.
Includes bibliographical references and index.
ISBN 978-1-57922-323-6 (cloth : alk. paper)
ISBN 978-1-57922-324-3 (pbk. : alk. paper)
ISBN 978-1-57922-719-7 (library networkable e-edition : alk. paper)
ISBN 978-1-57922-720-3 (consumer e-edition : alk. paper)
1. Education, Higher—Computer-assisted instruction.   2. Internet in higher education.
3. Blended learning.   I. Glazer, Francine S.
LB2395.7.B56   2012
371.3—dc23   2011017600

13-digit ISBN: 978-1-57922-323-6 (cloth)
13-digit ISBN: 978-1-57922-324-3 (paper)
13-digit ISBN: 978-1-57922-719-7 (library networkable e-edition)
13-digit ISBN: 978-1-57922-720-3 (consumer e-edition)

Printed in the United States of America

All first editions printed on acid free paper that meets the American National Standards Institute Z39-48 Standard.

Bulk Purchases

Quantity discounts are available for use in workshops and for staff development.
Call 1-800-232-0223

First Edition, 2012

10   9   8   7   6   5   4   3   2   1

For Beverley
Thank you for starting me along this path.

And for Richard
Thank you for the opportunity to continue.

Contents

Acknowledgments

This book would not have been possible without the contributions of many people. In particular, I'd like to thank the chapter authors—Alan Aycock, Elizabeth Barkley, Carl Behnke, Tracey Gau, and Robert Hartwell—for their essential contributions. It was a pleasure to work with each of them, and I have benefited from their ideas and experiences. James Rhem and Susan Slesinger, coeditors of the series, deserve special recognition for their vision, skillful editing, thoughtful comments on the manuscript, and their unflagging patience and constant encouragement.

Livingston Alexander, former provost of Kean University and current president of the University of Pittsburgh at Bradford, first encouraged me to explore online and blended learning and supported my work toward the master online teacher certificate from the Illinois Online Network (ION) of the University of Illinois. Were it not for his urging, I would still be numbered among the skeptics. Terry Fencl, Mary Wall, and particularly Tracey Smith, all instructors in the ION certificate program, not only taught and modeled best practices but took an active interest in the progression of my own online courses, offering encouragement and advice along the way.

Thanks to Michele Bertomen and Igor Matic, participants in the Faculty Writers' Circle at the New York Institute of Technology, who read drafts and suggested ways to restructure one of the chapters. Thanks also to Hattie Arnone, Denise Mancarella, and Nils Pearson. Special thanks to Meggin McIntosh, coach extraordinaire! And most of all, thank you, Harry, who helps me in so very many ways, and without whom this book would not have been completed.

Foreword

Not that long ago, the word "pedagogy" didn't occur very often in faculty conversations about teaching. Today, one hears it frequently. Without putting too much weight on the prominence of a single word, subtle shifts in discourse, in vocabulary, often do mark significant shifts in thinking, and faculty thinking about teaching has changed over the last several decades. Faculty have always wanted to teach well, wanted their students to learn and succeed, but for a very long time faculty have taught as they were taught; for the students who were like them in temperament and intelligence, the approach worked well enough. When only a highly filtered population of students sought higher education, the need to look beyond those approaches to teaching lay dormant. When a much larger and more diverse population began enrolling, the limits of traditional teaching emerged more sharply.

At the same time, intelligence itself became a more deeply understood phenomenon. Recognition of multiple kinds of intelligence—visual, auditory, kinesthetic, etc.—found wide acceptance, as did different styles of learning even within those different kinds of intelligence (as measured, for example, by the Myers-Briggs Type Indicator [MBTI] developed by Katharine Cook Briggs and Isabel Briggs Myers). Efforts to build ever more effective "thinking machines," that is to say, computers, through artificial intelligence sharpened understanding of how information needed to be processed in order for it to be assembled and utilized effectively. The seminal article, "Cognitive Apprenticeship: Teaching the Craft of Reading, Writing and Mathematics" was one by-product of this research, and one instructive aspect of this work lay in how it looked back to accumulated wisdom to lay its foundations for moving forward. Public schools had long dealt with large, diverse populations rather than highly filtered ones. Teachers there understood "scaffolding," "wait time," and "chunking" in conscious ways that were new to teachers at more advanced levels in education. Now, many of these terms, and more importantly these conscious and deliberate ways of thinking about teaching, have become commonplace in higher education.

Even more recently all this work has found support and expansion in the findings of neurobiological research into the human brain and how it operates, and in the study of groups and how they operate.

If renewed attention to teaching in higher education began as something of a "fix-it" shop approach aimed at helping individual faculty having problems with their teaching, it didn't stay that way very long. As Gaff and Simpson detail in their history of faculty development in the United States, pressure from the burgeoning "baby boom" population brought the whole business of university teaching up for reconsideration. What was relevance? What were appropriate educational goals, and what were the most effective means of meeting them? Traditionally, the primary expectation of faculty was that they remain current in their fields of expertise. Now, a whole new set of still forming expectations began to spring up on campuses all over the country.

Change often fails to come easily and smoothly. Generational and social conflicts, together with passionate political conflicts centering on the unpopular war in Vietnam, may have fueled the pressure for changes in teaching while making them more conflict-ridden than they needed to be. It is important to repeat: faculty have always wanted to teach well and have their students succeed. As the clouds of conflict from those decades have passed, the intellectual fruits have remained and grown. Some ascribe credit for change in faculty attitudes toward teaching to the social pressures of those decades. Whatever truth lies in that ascription, it seems equally clear that faculty's innate intellectual curiosity and eagerness to succeed in their life's work deserve as much credit, certainly for today's faculty interest in improved teaching.

Faculty face a challenge in embracing new understandings of effective teaching not unlike the challenge of any population of diverse intelligences in learning and applying new information. Some understanding emerging in the 1980s (in which much of the new thinking on teaching and learning began to appear) has cross-disciplinary, universal applicability, for example, the "Seven Principles of Good Practice in Higher Education" by Chickering and Gamson. But just as diverse people learn in diverse ways, diverse faculty will apply even universal principles in different ways, because both personalities and disciplinary cultures vary. Perhaps that is why many pedagogical insights into effective teaching have not aggregated into one universal, best way to teach. Instead, the forward-moving inquiry into effective teaching has spawned a variety of pedagogical approaches, each with strengths appropriate to particular teaching styles and situations.

While faculty today have greater curiosity about new understandings of effective ways to teach, they remain as cautious as anyone else about change. If they teach biology, they wonder how a particular approach might play out in teaching biology rather than how it works in teaching English literature. If they teach English literature, they may wonder if problem-based teaching (an approach highly effective in the sciences) has anything to offer their teaching and if anyone in their discipline has tried it. Every new idea requires translation and receives it in the hands of the next person to take it up and apply it in his or her work. And this is as it should be. Thus, this series of books strives to give faculty examples of new approaches to teaching as they are being applied in a representative sample of academic disciplines. In that, it extends the basic idea of The National Teaching and Learning Forum. For roughly 20 years, the central goal of Forum has been to offer faculty ideas in contexts: that is to say, to present them enough theory so that whatever idea about teaching and learning being discussed makes sense intellectually, but then to present that idea in an applied context. From this combination, faculty can see how an approach might fit in their own practice. Faculty do not need formulae; they need only to see ideas in contexts. They'll take it from there. And so our series of books offers faculty a multipaned window into a variety of nontraditional pedagogical approaches now being applied with success in different disciplines in higher education. Faculty will look in and find something of value for their own teaching. As I've said and believe with all my heart, faculty have always wanted to teach well and see their students succeed.

—James Rhem,
Executive Editor,
The National Teaching and Learning Forum

Introduction

Francine S. Glazer

Today's college students lead blended lives. In fact, if we loosely define the term *blended* to mean "partially virtual, partially tangible," then we can safely say all our lives have steadily become more and more blended. We access our news online, we pay bills online, we communicate through e-mail and social networks. People with Internet access go first to the web for information. We access the world via smartphones; why not access education that way too?

At its simplest, blended learning courses are those in which a significant amount of seat time, that is, time spent in the classroom, is replaced with online activities that involve students in meeting course objectives. Educause, a nonprofit organization whose mission is to promote the intelligent use of information technology in higher education, classifies courses based on the amount of time spent in each modality (Allen, Seaman, & Garrett, 2007). According to its classification scheme, blended courses have between 30% and 79% of activities online, face-to-face courses can include up to 29% of online activities, and fully online courses can include up to 20% of face-to-face activities.

Garrison and Vaughan (2008) define blended learning as "the thoughtful fusion of face-to-face and online learning experiences . . . such that the strengths of each are blended into a unique learning experience. . . . Blended learning is a fundamental redesign that transforms the structure of, and approach to, teaching and learning" (p. 5).

The unique characteristic of blended learning is that a significant portion of the activities occur in two areas: in person and online. Various other pedagogies—lecture, problem-based learning, Just-in-Time Teaching, cooperative learning, and others—can then be superimposed on the blended framework. The challenge of blended learning is to link, or blend, what happens in each medium so that face-to-face and online activities reinforce each other to create a single, unified, course.

1

A large body of literature, often categorized as the *no significant difference* literature, is often cited in support of the contention that there is no discernible benefit in the learning outcomes of students taught online compared to students taught in a face-to-face environment. In fact, careful meta-analyses of this literature reveal an important difference: Online learning, and in particular blended learning, can result in significantly better student learning compared to learning in the conventional classroom.

A meta-analysis conducted by the U.S. Department of Education (2009) winnowed down over 1,000 empirical studies to 51 that used a rigorous research design to measure student learning outcomes in both environments and provided sufficient information to allow calculation of an effect size. The finding was that students in fully online and blended courses tend to perform better than students in face-to-face courses, with students in blended courses performing significantly better. Another finding of the study was that the more time students spent on task, the greater the differential in student performance. These findings are attributable in part to active learning strategies, which include opportunities for reflection and interaction with peers, and in part to the enriched content that characterizes well-designed online and blended courses.

However, a significant caveat is in order: The studies in this meta-analysis do not demonstrate that online learning is superior regardless of how it is implemented. The combination of elements in the treatment conditions produced the observed benefits. In many of the studies showing an advantage for online learning, the online and classroom conditions differed in terms of time spent, curriculum, and pedagogy. The successful courses included additional learning time. Online and blended learning, lacking the time constraints imposed by face-to-face courses, are much more conducive to the expansion of learning time (U.S. Department of Education [2009] p. xvii). The successful courses also included more interactive materials (learning objects) and additional opportunities for collaboration.

In another meta-analysis of the literature, Zhao, Lei, Yan, Lai, and Tan (2005) identified three types of interactions—instructor and students, students and their peers, and students and content—as essential elements in determining the efficacy of a course's design. They further stated that courses with synchronous and asynchronous components—for example, blended courses—report more positive outcomes than courses that are entirely synchronous or entirely asynchronous. When the design of the various studies is teased apart, it's possible to group subsets that identify specific variables. Three components of online learning stand out as contributing to more effective learning: discourse, via discussion boards, blogs, or other media; reflection, either public or private; and writing to learn strategies.

To summarize, blended learning courses employ active learning strategies through the use of a variety of pedagogical approaches. The asynchronous nature of the blended component of the courses has the salutary effect of expanding the time students spend on course material. Discussions conducted online encourage reflection and usually reach 100% participation. As a result, the face-to-face time can be used more effectively, with students extending the material beyond what might be achieved in a conventional face-to-face course. The students in a blended course make more and richer connections between what they are learning and what they already know, creating a robust scaffold to organize the information. The following sections contain a more detailed look at some of the characteristics of successful blended learning courses.

BLENDED LEARNING DEMANDS ACTIVE LEARNING

Blended learning not only supports active learning by students, it demands it. Effective blended learning courses require students to interact with each other, the content, and their own thoughts. Students need a way to not only take in information but also to process it: checking their understanding, organizing their knowledge, and making connections with what they already know (Ambrose, Bridges, DiPietro, Lovett, & Norman, 2010; Svinicki, 2004).

Blended learning that incorporates active learning strategies provides students with vehicles to help them do just that. One of the strengths of blended learning is that it combines synchronous and asynchronous methodologies. Zhao et al. (2005) established that a course combining synchronous and asynchronous elements propels students to greater learning than they might have achieved in a face-to-face or a fully online course.

It's important to remember that *asynchronous* does not mean *passive*. Many interactive techniques lend themselves to synchronous and asynchronous modes. Because students spend so much of their free time online, blended courses have the potential to engage students in a way that a conventional course cannot, providing them with repeated opportunities to review information and practice skills in a comfortable environment.

BLENDED LEARNING SUPPORTS NUMEROUS PEDAGOGICAL APPROACHES

Blended learning offers the opportunity to design a course in multiple ways. Some faculty members use the online portion for students to work independently, learning facts and concepts, and the face-to-face time for them to work collaboratively on more demanding tasks. Other faculty members incorporate collaboration in the online portion of the course, taking advantage of its asynchronous nature to allow students to work in teams without having to find a common time to meet. In either scheme, student interaction is increased compared to the conventional lecture/test/lecture/test rhythm often prevalent in a course.

Many well-established pedagogical approaches can be successfully employed in a blended course: cooperative learning (Johnson, Johnson, & Smith, 1991; Millis, 2010; Millis & Cottell, 1997), team-based learning (Michaelson, Knight, & Fink, 2004; Michaelson, Sweet, & Parmelee, 2009), Just-in-Time Teaching (Novak, Gavrin, Christian, & Patterson, 1999; Simkins & Maier, 2009), problem-based and case-based learning (Amador, Miles, & Peters, 2007; Buck Institute for Education, n.d.; Duch, Groh, & Allen, 2001), simulations (Hertel & Millis, 2002), and more. It is important to note that using groups online is one way to build a learning community in that environment, which is an essential element of making it attractive to students.

Collaborative work benefits from the ability to meet asynchronously. The built-in time for reflection inherent to an asynchronous environment can facilitate deeper and more profound thinking in a way that a synchronous conversation does not. Web-based supplemental resources are immediately at hand, without the need to visit the library or tutoring center. Furthermore, it is often less disruptive to the group's work to access these materials in an asynchronous online environment than it would be if everyone were sitting together at a computer. And, speaking purely logistically, students can work collaboratively on projects without having to find a common time and place.

BLENDED LEARNING CREATES TIME

One of the unexpected benefits of blended learning is that it has the effect of creating time. Today's college students spend so much time online in so many aspects of their lives, it doesn't necessarily register with them that work done online for class is time spent on their studies. Learning objects that feel like games, such as those discussed by Tracey Gau in Chapter 4, engage students in learning by making it enjoyable.

One of the courses discussed by Carl Behnke in Chapter 1, a travel-learn course, provides an excellent illustration of this concept. Typical travel-learn courses often surround traveling to another country with 1 to 2 weeks of intense preparation and a week of wrap-up activities. Carl leveraged the blended format to give his students more extensive preparation before traveling. Extending the preparatory period over several weeks enabled him to require his students to conduct in-depth research on the location and topics they were studying. As a result, their experiences on-site were richer and more meaningful than they had been prior to the addition of the blended component of the course.

BLENDED LEARNING COURSES MUST BE LAYERED

It is therefore critical that the two are clearly interdependent, with each one adding substantial learning value to the course. Good instructional design is vitally important to the success of a blended learning course, perhaps even more so than in a traditional classroom or in fully online courses. The move to blended learning gives the faculty member an opportunity to revisit his or her course's instructional design. One of the pitfalls unique to blended learning courses is that students will not see the online and the face-to-face components as equal in value and will therefore spend most or all their time and effort in only one of the two modalities.

I like to think of this interdependence between online and face-to-face as *layering* the content. It's important to direct the students' attention in such a way that they see the need to attend to what happens in the classroom and the online environment. If activities extend from online to face-to-face and back again, if participation is required in both places, if student work is turned in online and in the classroom, and—perhaps most important of all—if the instructor is visible in both places giving students feedback on their performance and moderating the discussions, then a course is layered well.

Chatfield (2010) describes two ways to think about layering courses, which she terms *front loading* and *back loading*. In a front-loaded course, students are exposed to most or all of the content prior to the face-to-face class meeting. The assumption behind this strategy is that students will arrive at the face-to-face setting with some familiarity with the topic, and will be primed to take their learning to a new level of understanding. As you might imagine, this strategy works well with students who have a high degree of foundational knowledge coming into the course, who are comfortable with the material, and who can learn independently.

Back-loaded courses use the face-to-face meeting to introduce the content, providing an overview of the material and a framework for how it fits together. Students then work online to incorporate the details and elaborate on the concepts. Chatfield (2010) recommends this strategy for introductory courses, in which students might need more help in building a conceptual framework.

Layering works best when both parts of the course are designed for active learning. Think about it for a moment: If the online environment is designed to facilitate students' intake of information and there are no opportunities for interaction, then how can the students demonstrate their grasp of the material to the instructor or to themselves? The problem we face then is deciding where to put each activity. For example, discussions can take place in class and online. Will participants in a particular discussion benefit more from a face-to-face environment with the immediacy that context offers, or online, taking advantage of the built-in time for reflection?

In Chapter 3, Aycock describes how he incorporates active learning into the online and face-to-face portions of his Survey of World Cultures course by beginning the discussions online in small groups of 8–10. Students present *entrance tickets*—short essays tied to the day's reading—upon arrival for the face-to-face portion of the class. This approach, online discussion followed by writing an essay, combines with others he describes to create a rich and sophisticated discussion in class that would not have occurred without the additional depth created by giving students the opportunity to reflect on the material alone, by writing the entrance ticket, and with peers through the online discussions.

BLENDED LEARNING GIVES EVERY STUDENT A VOICE

When you think of an in-class discussion, what image comes to mind? Frequently, faculty will describe a situation in which a small number of students dominate the discussion, some listening attentively and speaking occasionally, and others nodding sagely and looking interested. It's relatively easy for a student to participate by looking interested and contributing small comments that don't add much substance to the discussion. Sometimes a faculty member includes class participation as a grading criterion, which raises the question: How do you track, let alone evaluate, class participation?

Many strategies encourage more student participation, such as the widely used think-pair-share technique (Lyman, 1981). Students first think through the question, and then discuss it with a partner. When the entire class discusses the material, each student has rehearsed his or her ideas with a peer, and many more students are comfortable participating. Even so, the immediacy of the in-class discussion favors students who can easily articulate their thoughts. Outspoken students can often intimidate the quieter students, even if that's not their intent. In my own classroom, I frequently see a quiet student whom I know has the right information hesitate to speak, even though the group is headed in the wrong direction.

When discussions take place online, though, the students who need time to reflect can take that time and then post their thoughts on the site. Asynchronous discussions level the playing field. Even if the students who are quick to speak in class post their comments quickly, the quieter students can still add their ideas and participate fully in the conversation. Students who are unsure of how best to express themselves can rehearse and proofread their responses—a luxury that doesn't exist in the face-to-face setting. Students who don't like others' eyes on them when they speak can share their ideas in relative privacy—no one else can see or hear them.

One more advantage of asynchronous discussions is it's harder to lurk. Students can no longer nod sagely and look interested; to visibly participate, they must contribute. As a result, it is much easier to approach 100% class participation as students post and respond to one another (Bender, 2003). Additionally, the discussion generally lasts longer than a typical class session. The added time for idea incubation helps students make more connections between the new material and prior knowledge.

BLENDED LEARNING MAXIMIZES THE VALUE OF FACE-TO-FACE TIME

When done well, blended learning combines the best attributes of face-to-face and online courses. Face-to-face contact time is available for synchronous give-and-take, thrashing out questions about difficult topics, identifying and resolving students' assumptions and misconceptions about a topic, building community, doing hands-on activities, and addressing any questions students may have about the technology.

Some of the chapters in this book describe courses in which the face-to-face time was used to accomplish *more*—deeper discussions, higher-level cognitive tasks, integration of material. Gau's course described in Chapter 4 includes a large class meeting to set the stage for each unit, after which students work online, using interactive learning objects to gauge their mastery of the material and discussing it with their classmates. Smaller discussion sections then take place face-to-face, and students "debate, discuss, collaborate, and make presentations on the material" (p. 91). Rather than using face-to-face time to summarize and interpret the readings, Gau engages her students in higher-level cognitive tasks—analysis, evaluation, synthesis.

Similarly, in Chapter 2 I discuss an activity used in an upper-level genetics course, in which teams of students work online to gather, share, and evaluate information in preparation for a face-to-face debate. By working online as a team, students not only learn the material, they learn each others' areas of strength. When they debate in class, the teams know almost instinctively which student should argue a specific point.

BLENDED LEARNING HELPS STUDENTS ORGANIZE THEIR KNOWLEDGE

Svinicki (2004) points out that one of the most effective things we can do as instructors to help our students encode information in their long-term memories is help them build an organizational structure for the material: "It is worth your while as an instructor to spend time thinking organizationally about your course's content and to design instruction around that organization" (p. 31). Well-organized knowledge is easier to connect to prior knowledge, and therefore easier to retrieve when needed.

Blended learning can be used in such a way that it makes explicit the task of organizing the knowledge. For example, the written talking points each student group prepared online in my biology course provided a means not only to collect information but also to structure it in a way that made the relevant information easy to find during the face-to-face mediation. The learning objects used in Gau's literature course described in Chapter 4 helped students prepare for more complex tasks by helping them review information and sequence it correctly.

The products students generate as they organize their knowledge can then be used in face-to-face settings to help students form a richer set of connections between new material and prior knowledge. In Chapter 3 Aycock describes the use of written assignments, completed, submitted, and discussed online, as prompts for discussion in the face-to-face sessions, and illustrates how these written pieces enable the students to move beyond what they might have done in a conventional course.

BLENDED LEARNING ENCOURAGES SELF-DIRECTED LEARNING

Blended courses can be designed so that students can explore specific subtopics in greater depth even as they fulfill course requirements. For example, one strategy might be to give each student in the class a unique discussion question to answer, and then require that he or she replies to two or three peers. Another strategy might be to require students to identify an external resource germane to the class and post a link with a description of the resource and a brief analysis of its value. These types of activities allow students to personalize the material to better suit their interests while maintaining a standard set of activities for all students. Blended learning courses can also include online tutorials for students who need to brush up on their skills or prior knowledge, links to additional resources, and additional activities for students who desire more practice or want more challenges.

Contract learning (see, for example, Weimer, 2002) is another strategy that has been used successfully, although it adds another layer of complexity to the course design. Students are presented with a menu of activities and are given the freedom to select what they will do to fulfill course requirements. Hartwell and Barkley's Chapter 5 explores how to take that approach one step further—their course allows students to choose not only the activities they will complete but whether they will do so in an online, blended, or face-to-face setting.

Lifelong learning is an essential skill for today's graduates and one that is prized by employers. Blended learning helps students develop the desire and the skills to continue learning throughout their lives by giving students more control over their learning and teaching them the skills they need to acquire, organize, and incorporate new information into their understanding of the world. The chapters in this book explore five courses in detail as the authors describe course context, their pedagogical strategies, and lessons learned.

Carl Behnke, author of Chapter 1, is an assistant professor of hospitality and tourism management at Purdue University. Quantity Food Preparation is a midsize (80–100 students), sophomore-level course required of students in the hospitality program. Traditionally, cooking is taught using an apprenticeship model; moving to a blended format presents challenges comparable to those in any technical, studio, or laboratory course. The students in this particular hospitality program don't think they'll ever cook and are much more interested in what happens in the front of the hotel. They often don't purchase the textbook, let alone use it, and they need external motivators. Carl describes the evolution of his traditional lecture-and-demonstration course into a blended course: He has incorporated tutorials, writing assignments, and assessments in the online component of his course, and the face-to-face component is highly interactive. His design model is predicated on the idea that the online environment works well for factual learning, while face-to-face is better suited for working at the higher levels of Bloom's taxonomy. Carl also discusses how he uses blended learning as part of a travel-learn course, which increases what students learn and enhances their experience when they travel to the site.

In Chapter 2, I explore the use of case studies in a blended format. Principles of Genetics is a content-heavy undergraduate course that requires students to use a different skill set from what they are used to using in their science courses. As the activity progresses, students share their research in online discussions and collaborate to create the materials used in the face-to-face sessions that are the culmination of the case study. I share the students' reactions and their suggestions about how to improve the activity, many of which I incorporated the following semester.

Alan Aycock is acting director of the University of Wisconsin–Milwaukee's Learning Technology Center and an instructor in the Department of Anthropology. The course he describes in Chapter 3, Survey of World Cultures, is a midsize (80–100 students) course that fulfills a general education distribution requirement for students. In addition to switching to a blended approach, Alan went from a small number of high-stakes assessments to a large number—between 30 and 50—of low-stakes assessments throughout the semester. Students complete much of each unit online, using face-to-face sessions to debrief and close the loop on their learning. Entrance and exit assignments for each unit, combined with rapid feedback from Alan, enable students to develop their ideas throughout each unit so their experience is, as he describes it, "richer and more rewarding" (p. 73). One challenge he discusses is how to give a large class a sense of community; another is how to sustain a discussion on a topic first online, then face-to-face, as the students progress from lower to higher cognitive levels in their thinking.

Tracey Gau is a faculty fellow and senior course designer at the Center for Learning Enhancement, Assessment, and Redesign at the University of North Texas. In Chapter 4 she describes her World Literature I class, a midsize (150 students) required general education class. The online component of this course is designed to help students master the factual material; they use learning objects and quizzes to gauge their comprehension. Tracey eloquently describes how learning objects, which at a casual glance look simple, can be very effective in stimulating long-term recall and application of content. The course is highly interactive online and in class, with students participating in online discussions by responding to a variety of question prompts. Tracey presents an interesting model of how to make a large class feel small so the students develop a sense of community in their online discussions.

The community extends to the classroom, where the discussions become more analytical.

Chapter 5 coauthors Robert Hartwell, professor of music history, and Elizabeth Barkley, professor of music, coteach a course at Foothill College. *Music of Multicultural America* is a large class (350 students) with a different instructional design model—a learning contract. In the learning contract model, many more learning activities are available than are required. This course is unique in that students have the option of taking the course fully face-to-face, fully online, or fully blended. The schedule of face-to-face presentations is published in advance so students can choose which class sessions they want to attend. Out-of-class activities are also available as options, and these activities are quite different from what happens in the face-to-face class, but they meet the same learning goals. One interesting result of this technique is the different mix of students in each face-to-face meeting; Robert and Elizabeth describe how they approach creating a sense of community when each community is different. Another issue they address is how to design the course so students have the freedom to tailor it to their own interests and schedule while still meeting course goals and objectives.

The chapters in this book contain examples of specific courses and frank discussions of the challenges unique to each course. Each author used blended learning differently to address those challenges, so five different types of course design are presented. Blended learning is a flexible pedagogical tool that can be used in many different disciplines and implemented in as many different ways to engage students and enhance their learning. I hope these examples will spark your imagination as you contemplate your own courses.

REFERENCES

Allen, I. E., Seaman, J., & Garrett, R. (2007). *Blending in: The extent and promise of blended education in the United States*. Needham, MA: Sloan Consortium. Retrieved from http://sloanconsortium.org/sites/default/files/Blending_In.pdf

Amador, J. A., Miles, L., & Peters, C. B. (2007). *The practice of problem-based learning: A guide to implementing PBL in the college classroom*. Bolton, MA: Anker.

Ambrose, S. A., Bridges, M. W., DiPietro, M., Lovett, M. C., & Norman, M. K. (2010). *How learning works: Seven research-based principles for smart teaching*. San Francisco, CA: Jossey-Bass.

Bender, T. (2003). *Discussion-based online teaching to enhance student learning: Theory, practice and assessment*. Sterling, VA: Stylus.

Buck Institute for Education & Boise State University. (n.d.). *Project based learning: The online resource for PBL.* Retrieved from http://www.pbl-online.org/

Chatfield, K. (2010). *Content "loading" in hybrid/blended learning.* Retrieved from http://devsite2.sloanconsortium.org/effective_practices/content-quotloading quot-hybridblended-learning

Duch, B. J., Groh, S. E., & Allen, D. E. (2001). *The power of problem-based learning.* Sterling, VA: Stylus.

Garrison, D. R., & Vaughan, N. D. (2007). *Blended learning in higher education: Framework, principles, and guidelines.* San Francisco, CA: Jossey-Bass.

Hertel, J. P., & Millis, B. (2002). *Using simulations to promote learning in higher education: An introduction.* Sterling, VA: Stylus.

Johnson, D. J., Johnson, R., & Smith, K. J. (1991). *Active learning: Cooperation in the college classroom.* Edina, MN: Interaction.

Lyman, F. (1981). The responsive classroom discussion. In A. S. Anderson, (Ed.), *Mainstreaming digest* (pp. 109–113). College Park: University of Maryland Press.

Michaelson, L. K., Knight, A., & Fink, D. (Eds.). (2004). *Team-based learning: A transformative use of small groups in college teaching.* Sterling, VA: Stylus.

Michaelsen, L. K., Sweet, M., & Parmelee, D. X. (Eds.). (2009). Team-based learning: Small group learning's next big step. *New Directions for Teaching and Learning,* (116).

Millis, B. J. (Ed.). (2010). *Cooperative learning in higher education: Across the disciplines, across the academy.* Sterling, VA: Stylus.

Millis, B. J., & Cottell, P. G., Jr. (1997). *Cooperative learning for higher education faculty.* Phoenix, AZ: Oryx Press.

Novak, G., Gavrin, A., Christian, W., & Patterson, E. (1999). *Just-in-time teaching: Blending active learning with web technology.* Upper Saddle River, NJ: Prentice Hall.

Simkins, S., & Maier, M. (Eds.). (2009). *Just-in-time teaching: Across the disciplines, across the academy.* Sterling, VA: Stylus.

Svinicki, M. D. (2004). *Learning and motivation in the postsecondary classroom.* Bolton, MA: Anker.

U.S. Department of Education. (2009). *Evaluation of evidence-based practices in online learning: A meta-analysis and review of online learning studies.* Washington, DC: Author.

Weimer, M. (2002). *Learner-centered teaching: Five key changes to practice.* San Francisco, CA: Jossey-Bass.

Zhao, Y., Lei, J., Yan, B., Lai, C., & Tan, S. (2005). What makes the difference? A practical analysis of research on the effectiveness of distance education. *Teachers College Record, 107*(8), 1836–1834.

Blended Learning in the Culinary Arts
Tradition Meets Technology

Carl Behnke

"This course material is pertinent to my professional training." "Course assignments are interesting and stimulating." "My instructor has an effective style of presentation." When I started teaching, these statements were the most challenging line items on my course evaluations. My background and experience as a chef had prepared me to handle practically anything that could happen in a restaurant environment; however, it left me woefully unprepared for teaching.

It was 1998, and after 18 years of cooking in restaurant and hotel kitchens it was time for a career change. Positive experiences as a tutor and mentor to young culinarians led me to consider the idea of a becoming a culinary instructor. I didn't think the lack of formal educational training was an issue; after all, how hard could it be to teach? At the risk of bad puns and overused clichés, little did I know this was the proverbial out of the frying pan and into the fire situation.

Being a chef was familiar and easy. I began working in kitchens as a teenager, so cooking was second nature to me. However, being a teacher was a different story. As a chef, I was used to working in an intense, frantic environment with a small, close-knit team of cooks. As an instructor, I had to teach a classroom of up to 90 unmotivated sophomore students. I say "unmotivated" because students interested in pursuing a professional cooking career tend to enroll in associate's degree culinary programs. Our hospitality program is more broadly focused and designed to cultivate restaurant, hotel, and tourism managers, not chefs and cooks. Few if any of my students had a desire to cook for a living. In fact, it seemed many of them were intimidated by the very idea, and more than once I heard complaints about the professional relevance of my course and materials. This was my audience, and somehow I needed to teach them the fundamentals of cooking. To do this I knew I had to reach out and engage them, or my time as an instructor was likely limited.

Because I was a novice instructor, students were just one part of my challenge. The other challenge was the nature of the supporting course materials, in particular, a professional cookbook of more than 800 pages. Not only was I faced with the challenge of teaching an unmotivated audience, I had to use a very intimidating and expensive textbook to do it. Combine a lack of formal teacher training with an intimidating textbook and an unmotivated audience, and you have all the ingredients for a recipe for disaster. Before I go any further, some background details are in order.

The hospitality and tourism management program where I teach has an enrollment of about 500 undergraduate and 40 graduate students. Its curriculum is designed around the three emphasis areas of food service, lodging, and tourism management. Because of my background, I was assigned to teach about 90 students per semester in food service lab and lecture classes. The lecture class, HTM 291: Quantity Food Production, is a required course most undergraduate students take during their sophomore year. The course runs over a 15-week semester with 75-minute class meetings twice a week. At the sophomore level, most of my students don't really seem to know what they want to do when they graduate. Their responses to this question generally range from the generic "manager" to the more specific "wedding planner." However, while they may be unsure of what they will eventually do with their degree, I think it is safe to say that a strong majority of them would indicate they know what they don't want to do, and that is cook. My guess is that 70% or more of my students do not want to be in this class and don't think it is important. They are not a hostile audience, just an indifferent one. My challenge, therefore, was to tailor the course in such a way that it would be stimulating and motivating.

When the class was first turned over to me, the materials that accompanied it consisted of a two-inch stack of overheads, lecture notes, and several quizzes plus a midterm and final exam. I remember muddling my way through that first semester, more or less just reading from the overheads and notes. Readings were from the massive cookbook that was the assigned textbook, but I later learned that none of my students bought the book. During a heart-to-heart discussion with one of them, the student told me that since my quizzes and tests were straight from the overheads he didn't bother to read the assigned chapters. All he had to do was memorize the basic facts and figures from my overheads. Furthermore, it seemed this was the chosen method of study for most of the class; I was off to a less than stellar start. Change was in order, but it wouldn't be quick or painless. Over time, the class evolved in a way I now know is called *blended learning*, where the content is taught using face-to-face and online methods.

In this blended learning model, the face-to-face component consists primarily of lectures and demonstrations about the fundamentals of cooking methods, ingredients, and terminology, as well as operational issues associated with kitchen management (see Figure 1.1). Reading assignments are posted at the beginning of the semester and correspond to daily PowerPoint lectures. Additionally, culinary videos are shown periodically throughout the semester. The group project is divided into three deliverable components, including a written paper, creation of a culturally appropriate menu, and a concluding class presentation. Group activities are also conducted at various points during the semester, while traditional paper and pencil midterm and final exams are scheduled as appropriate.

The online component of the course includes three current events essay assignments and five tests. Additional online resources include tutorials, streaming videos, abbreviated lecture notes, supplemental worksheets, and video note sheets. The group project is assigned in class at the beginning of the semester and is supported online through the use of technology built into the learning management system, such as the Groups tool and e-mail.

I wish I could say that as I moved into the realm of blended learning I carefully considered the associated educational issues and followed a research-grounded approach; however, the reality is that it was more a matter of looking at my resources and abilities and selecting tasks that seemed achievable. As the class evolved, a pattern emerged. The easiest tasks to automate were those with clear-cut objective responses, such as multiple-choice tests. Subjective tasks, demanding opinion and independent thought, could still be done in an online format, but in fairness to the students, the grading could not be fully automated. I still had to review, offer feedback, and grade each submission. For these tasks, the technology was used as a means of asynchronous delivery and organization.

Another way to look at the division of tasks between online and face-to-face delivery methods comes from instructional design. The current taxonomy of educational objectives (Krathwohl, 2002), revised from Bloom's original taxonomy (Bloom, Engelhart, Furst, Hill, & Krathwohl, 1956), classifies knowledge into one of four categories (factual, conceptual, procedural, and metacognitive) that span six cognitive processes (remember, understand, apply, analyze, evaluate, and create). This taxonomy offers a two-dimensional tabular means of classifying course objectives and content.

When you look at course content in this manner, it is easy to see how online technology can be very useful for automating tasks that fall within the

Figure 1.1   Class Agenda

Date	Readings	Lecture	Online Assignment	In-Class Activity	Video	Group Project	Tests
1/8	Gisslen Chapter #1 & #2	Orientation: PPT: Intro to Quantity Food Production				Teams & Topics Assigned	
1/10	Gisslen Chapter #3 & #4	PPT: Basic Principles of Cooking & Equipment	Cooking Equipment tutorial released	Sanitation Scenario			
1/15					Principles & Processes of Cooking		
1/17	Gisslen Chapter #5	PPT: Recipe & Food Costing	Recipe Costing—post online worksheet			Demo of Cultural Presentation	Vista Test #1 Released @ 3PM
1/22	Gisslen Chapter #4	PPT: Menus	Basic Cooking Jeopardy	Menu Comparison		Begin F2F Group Meetings	
1/24	Gisslen Chapter #21	PPT: Breakfast, Beverages and Service Styles			Basic Kitchen Preparation (begin)		Vista Test #1 Closes @ 1PM
1/29	Gisslen Chapter #7 & #8	PPT: Mise en Place		Understanding and Developing Flavor	Basic Kitchen Preparation (continue)		
1/31	Gisslen Chapter #10	PPT: Meats	OA #1: Global Food—released @ 3PM		Basic Kitchen Preparation (finish)		Vista Test #2 Released @ 3PM
2/5	Gisslen Chapter #11	PPT: Preparing Meats	Fabrication and Yield Analysis released			Group Project Updates	
2/7	Gisslen Chapter #12	Global Food Presentation	OA #1: Due by 3PM	Global Food Discussion	Purchasing Meat		Vista Test #2 Closes @ 1PM
2/12	Gisslen Chapter #13	PPT: Poultry		Product Utilization			
2/14	Gisslen	PPT: Seafood	Poultry Jeopardy			2-page cultural	

dimensions of remember and understand but more challenging when trying to teach material within the dimensions of evaluate and create. Because answers to these types of tasks are not clear cut, interpretation on the part of the instructor is required. My course has evolved in such a manner that most of the online resources are geared toward the basic remember and understand dimensions, reserving the lecture for the higher-order tasks of analyzing and evaluating. Since students learn in different ways and at different paces, placing the rote knowledge tasks online allows students the freedom of asynchronous, self-directed study. I then use the face-to-face class time to elaborate on the basic foundational knowledge acquired either online or from the textbook. I have found that teaching in this fashion seems to work by making the class more flexible, approachable, and intrinsically motivating, perhaps because of the self-directed nature of the online materials.

I want to elaborate on one point regarding the term *blended learning*. Simply posting course content online or automating a subset of the course interactions does not blend a class. Much of the literature defines blended learning as an effective integration of distance education and face-to-face methods developed with the goal of leveraging the best elements of both techniques (Chen & Jones, 2007; Garrison & Kanuka, 2004; Mortera-Gutiérrez, 2006; Osguthorpe & Graham, 2003). The key points are *effective integration* and *leveraging the best of both techniques*. I am concerned when I see instructors interpret the online learning component in a superficial manner, posting materials such as presentations or notes on the Internet and never specifically referring to them again in the face-to-face setting. It seems the expectation is that simply posting content for asynchronous access will cause students to embrace the technique and deal with the material, thus making life easier on the teacher. To me, this is more aptly described as parallel learning, since the two forms of content do not actually merge as one would expect from something called blended. To truly be blended, the various means and media delivering the content must be brought together in complementary and reinforcing roles. The reality is that blended learning does not necessarily make life easier for the instructor. In fact the time demands associated with properly developing, implementing, and maintaining a blended learning course are the same, and perhaps greater, than those associated with teaching a traditional face-to-face class, a point that I explore later in this chapter.

In terms of my Quantity Food Production course, you might ask where did I begin? The first step was to seek a new textbook and supporting course materials. It turns out that soon after I began teaching, the author of the

800-page textbook published an abbreviated textbook, designed as an introduction to cooking rather than as a professional culinary bible. This, as they
say, was a no-brainer. The students didn't need to know how to make souf-
flés when the goal was to teach them how to scramble eggs. Since many of
our students grew up in the multimedia environment of TV, computers,
video games, movies, cell phones, and MP3 players, I began to seek out
appropriate multimedia materials. These can be quite expensive, so it took
some time, but eventually I acquired several professionally produced videos
and DVDs on culinary and restaurant operations.

The next step that needed addressing was my teaching style. Having had
no formal educational training or experience, I wasn't equipped with any
teaching tools. However, I have always been interested in computers and the
Internet, so through colleagues and mentors I began to learn about concepts
such as asynchronous teaching, constructivism, and scaffolding, and tools
such as WebCT, Blackboard, and streaming video. I started with the basics,
first keeping an online grade book and posting my presentations, later moving to online assignments, tests, streaming videos, and group projects. I also
worked at changing my lecturing methods. As a student, I never learned well
from teachers who read from slides or simply regurgitated the textbook; yet
as a novice teacher, more than once I found myself making these very mis-
takes. I decided that if I was going to engage the students, I needed to bring
some life into the class by leveraging my experiences as a chef. Imagine for
yourself how the students perk up during a lecture on knife safety when I
show them my scars and relate the stories behind each one. Or during a
lecture on the importance of banquet production and planning I tell them
about the time I ran out of soup during a wedding banquet and had to make
more in less than five minutes. Incorporating real-life experiences into my
lectures became one of the more successful ways of motivating students and
stimulating dialogue.

Motivating students: I have come to believe this is one of the most difficult, yet most important, challenges a teacher faces because students differ in
so many ways. Every student applies a unique filter when interpreting the
material being taught. I say "unique" because this filter develops through
one's specific interactions with and perspectives of life: Is the student male
or female? Raised in a rural or urban setting? Brought up in wealth or pov-
erty? Has brothers and sisters or is an only child? Extroverted or introverted?
Also, it is important to remember these filters are constantly changing. Every
experience has an impact. In fact, it could be argued that students' filters are
subjected to more changes than most other people's because they are at a

point in their lives where they are experiencing a significant degree of independence and the consequences related to their decisions. Every educational encounter, opinion, and activity leads to vivid impressions, positive and negative, which in turn are integrated into their filters and subsequent behaviors.

These are just a few of the characteristics that contribute to these unique filters. I am sure you can think of many more. The point is that each student will interact with educational content differently. Today I know this is part of a philosophical concept called *constructivism*, a philosophy I keep in mind as I continue to revise my courses. If you wish to explore this philosophy further, Phillips (1995) provides a good starting point, offering a concise overview of the differing perspectives of constructivism. In terms of education, one size does not fit all, especially when filtered in such unique ways. Motivating students, in my opinion, is one of the keys to involving them in the learning process. Students who are motivated enough to actively engage with the material will assume responsibility for learning.

To develop course materials and methods that are intrinsically motivating, one must begin with an understanding of each student's unique nature. Thorpe (2002) argues that dynamic interpersonal interaction is necessary to reflectively respond to an individual's needs. In a large class setting, getting to know students and giving them the opportunity for personalized interactions can be a challenge; therefore, I choose to use as many instructional methods as possible, or at least as realistically possible, in a shotgun approach to teaching. Over time and through trial and error, my teaching toolbox has grown from basic lectures, overheads, and demonstrations to include digital media such as PowerPoint presentations, videos, online tutorials and tests, and even games like Team Jeopardy. My personal experience is that variety is associated with engagement and, ultimately, greater satisfaction for my students and me.

Motivating students begins with the instructional design process. Keller (1999) noted that instructional design intended for use in a classroom setting is different from instructional design intended for use in a self-directed learning environment. In a face-to-face setting, an instructor can adapt to students' needs as soon as they get a feel for the situation; however, in an online course, students will often be interacting with content in the absence of the instructor. There is no way for the instructor to get a feel for the students' needs in this situation without some form of personal, direct communication. So how does one go about motivating students in a blended learning environment that combines both of these settings?

New technology, new teaching techniques, and new materials: It was a new beginning. The next challenge was to weave it all together into a coherent course structure that motivated an indifferent audience. As mentioned earlier, I began by posting assignments and presentations online; however, I soon learned that without face-to-face reinforcement, the lessons were not sinking in. It seemed the students quickly discovered that the online materials were supplemental. The old saying, "You can't expect what you don't inspect," was in play. Once the students came to perceive the online materials as optional, they stopped using them. I had to get out of this parallel mode and truly integrate the online and lecture content. In other words, blending was required.

As an example of how I blend online learning with the face-to-face classroom, in one of my current online assignments, Restaurants and Nutrition, I require students to read three industry articles related to the hot topics of nutritional awareness, obesity, and restaurant responsibility. Once the students have read the articles, which are posted online, they are expected to submit a short essay starting with one of the following statements: (a) Restaurants should publicize their menu items' nutritional values because . . . , or (b) Restaurants should not be required to publicize their menu items' nutritional values because. . . . Students' grades are based in part on their ability to take a stance and support it using the literature provided.

This assignment is released according to the agenda, and students are given one week to complete their essay, which they submit online. Reading through the essays allows me to take note of student opinions. Once I go through the first 40 or so essays, I notice distinct patterns emerging. These patterns and opinions become critical in the next stage when they are blended into the face-to-face lecture.

As previously mentioned, reinforcing online assignments in the face-to-face setting is critical; in fact, this is the blending of blended learning. Because of this, when I assign a task, such as the online essay assignment, I schedule the supporting lecture about one week after the essay's due date. This way, students' memory of the topic is still relatively fresh. During this class session, I use a PowerPoint presentation to give the students more facts and figures, thus reinforcing and expanding their understanding of the issues. Finally, I start a discussion with questions (sometimes provocative or sensational) based upon the patterns and opinions I noted while grading the essays. When all goes as planned, a vigorous debate starts and the class comes alive. To me, this is when learning is truly blended, when material is presented and reinforced through the use of different but complementary means and methods.

Developing a blended learning course is somewhat similar to planning a dinner. It begins with the overall goal: providing a memorable event for your guests. Specific objectives leading to this goal may include planning the menu and determining the guest list. Some activities supporting these objectives include purchasing the ingredients and preparing the various dishes, of course, which are timed appropriately so your guests are treated to a fine meal. Once the meal has ended, guests have departed, and the kitchen has been cleaned, you then reflect on the event and consider what you might do differently in the future. Your task as instructor is to take a similar logical approach beginning with the overall goals. What would you expect for your students to be able to accomplish upon completion of the course? From there you need to consider specific objectives and how you intend to assess attainment. The next step is to develop instructional activities that logically support your objectives and assessments. Once these pieces are in place, it is time to teach. To use another saying commonly heard in kitchens, "Plan your work, then work your plan!" After administering your instructional activities and assessments, it is time to reflect. Reflecting upon performance, yours and your students', involves a critical analysis of your goals, objectives, activities, and assessments. This is no different from planning any course; however, with a blended learning course, you have the added complication of considering which lesson plan activities best leverage the face-to-face and online advantages. Do these components complement or conflict? Does your course have a logical flow with online content supporting and supplementing face-to-face content in a timely fashion? Over time, a cycle emerges: goal, objective, activities, assess, reflect, revise, and repeat.

My online tests are another example of blended learning. Even though they are called *tests*, the term is somewhat of a misnomer. I really use them as a means of reinforcing course content in an objective and automatable manner. Most learning management systems allow you to design a fairly powerful test with numerous options, such as true/false, multiple choice, short answer, matching, or essay questions. Admittedly, given the asynchronous and remote nature of an online exam, it is easy for students to cheat by collaborating. While there are technological ways to combat this issue, I choose to use a different approach. I actually encourage my students to collaborate; the tests are open book, open notes, and even open friend. I use the tests more to ensure that students are studying the course materials outside the classroom environment than to assess knowledge gained. However, to keep them on their toes, I set up the tests with alternative questions. For example, imagine you are collaborating with a fellow student, John, on your test. You go to a computer lab with your notes and books, sit side by side and proceed to log on to the class site. John opens the test and begins. He gets his first question, which reads, "According to the Basic Kitchen Preparation video, a classic mirepoix is made from _____." This is a multiple-choice question with four possible responses. You open your test and move to your first question. However, since this is a question set with several alternatives, your question is different; it reads, "True/False: From the Basic Kitchen Preparation video, we know that dry rubs are used as flavor enhancers." So even though you are collaborating with John, your test will randomly offer questions that are different from his.

Another thing I do with these tests is to word the questions very specifically. The questions in the preceding example refer to notes taken from a specific video viewed in class. Other questions cite the lecture notes or textbook author. The students are informed from the beginning that acceptable responses must come from the source indicated. This reduces the chance of conflicting messages, which sometimes occurs when you have multiple sources of information, and simultaneously requires students to review their notes and read the chapters. In the case of this class, it is easy to see how the tests are used for reinforcing content as well as for assessing knowledge gain. My goal is to keep them thinking about the topic beyond the parameters of the classroom. Assessment of knowledge gain occurs during the midterm and final exams, which are taken independently in a face-to-face context.

This class has evolved in the direction of blended learning, but I am sure this is not the only workable approach. If I had the facility and resources to conduct this lecture as if it were a cooking show with daily cooking demonstrations and tastings, I think I might engage even more students. However, this approach is expensive and more appropriate in a culinary school dedicated to training cooks and chefs than in a hospitality program where the cooking is a small part of a much bigger picture. This is an important point: Your choice of teaching method(s) depends upon your audience, your resources, and your abilities. Transforming a class can be an exciting, but also intimidating, process that is not necessarily quick, easy, or painless. Were I to do it all over again, I would begin with a detailed appraisal of the current class and targeted audience, identify the goals and objectives, and then critically assess the media and methods currently in use. It wouldn't surprise me if I had to start over from scratch, because in my experience, classes often evolve as a series of hand-me-downs. As instructors move on to new and different courses, they often pass their notes and methods on to their replacement, who likely being already overwhelmed, latches on to these materials as if they were a lifeline. Over time they add and subtract material until eventually they move on, and the cycle repeats. I would guess that much of the material being taught today originated several generations of instructors ago, which may be fine in some cases. However, properly leveraging today's technology requires more than simply posting traditional content online. You must assess the needs of all stakeholders and the limitations of materials and technology. Finally, having taken the leap into blended learning, you must constantly gauge the effectiveness of your approach with measures such as course evaluations, qualitative interviews, and student grades, and then revise as necessary. Remember, technology is constantly changing, and if you are considering adopting a blended learning approach, you will need to stay abreast of the changes. Offering online components can be very demanding, but with time and experience, it can also be quite rewarding.

Is this process any different from developing or modifying a traditional face-to-face course? If you look beyond the obvious technological differences, it really isn't. A teacher who wishes to avoid classroom complacency must go through a similar development process. New technology is constantly being introduced in the classroom, so instructors need to stay up-to-date with these changes as well. The nature and needs of your students are constantly evolving, demanding flexibility on your part, and organizational goals are frequently revised, once again changing how you teach. So while the learning and implementation curve may not be as steep in the face-to-face classroom as it is with online technology and instruction, it still exists.

One challenge unique to technology is its fluid and dynamic nature. Every year brings new software and hardware to be mastered. Additionally, students have differing levels of access to technology. While my class is geared for sophomores, I have my share of juniors and seniors because of scheduling constraints. A senior may be using a computer that he or she purchased as a freshman four years earlier, likely loaded with original operating systems and software. By contrast, a sophomore might be using a computer that is just over a year old with more recent software. Yet another student may rely on university computer labs, which are constantly updated with the latest technology, while you as the instructor are working with a computer and software that could fall anywhere in between. In consideration of student access, your online component must be designed for the lowest technological common denominator, or else accommodations must be made for students with challenges related to accessibility or current technology.

Not too long ago, I encountered this very problem. Microsoft had introduced the latest version of its popular Office software, which usually came bundled with new computers. Students with these computers were submitting their group presentations to be uploaded on the course website; however, the new software was conflicting with the Blackboard course software and the older operating system still used in classroom computers. Students trying to show these presentations in class were unable to open them and had to resave the files in an older format. It was a minor issue that resolved itself as the older software was phased out, but it does illustrate the need to consider technology and students' degree of access when developing online materials.

In an ideal world, technology does what it is designed to do, no more and no less. It doesn't think outside the box nor does it interpret; everything is essentially black and white. People, on the other hand, are quite the opposite. We often do the unexpected and use technology in unanticipated manners; with people, most things are a shade of gray. What this means is that the instructor must provide the flexibility the technology lacks. For example, what do you do if Internet access fails during a test? In my case, I choose to give the students the benefit of the doubt and reopen or extend the test for the same duration that access was denied. What about disabled students? Every semester I have students with documented disabilities requiring extended testing time or similar adaptations. Depending upon your course management system, you may have to get creative when accommodating their needs. For instance, when I have a student with extended time requirements, I make a duplicate test that I release just to that student. At the same time, to prevent confusion, I have to restrict the student's access to the original test to avoid having two identical tests show up on his or her course home page. Technological challenges arise when individualizing to meet specific students' needs, which is why flexibility is essential; students should not be penalized for hardware and software limitations. The key is to become comfortable with online and computer-based tools. Once familiar with them, you will find their challenges are not that different from those you experience daily in a face-to-face environment.

This brings up the issue of technology support. If you intend to spend the time and money adopting an online approach, you need to be sure your institution supports your efforts in terms of time and money. It would be wasteful to go to the trouble of cultivating online materials if your school's administration has not made an ongoing commitment to support blended learning. Also, you must have ready access to tech support and confidence in the stability of your computer networks. Imagine what it would be like for you if the network crashed during a timed assignment and student submissions were lost, or if you kept all your grades in an online grade book only to have the server go down. Reliable tech support and regular course backups are real stress relievers. Finally, your competence with technology directly affects your comfort level in creating and managing the online aspects of a blended course. In my case, I took the hard path of trial and error to teach myself how to use these tools effectively, and you may or may not wish to follow that example. Alternative paths might include taking classes that bring you up to speed on the latest and greatest in technology or participating in professional development seminars related to advances in teaching and technology. Another possibility would be to find a mentor who has already developed and administered a blended learning course, and see if you can audit his or her class to cultivate a student's perspective. A combination of all three of these approaches should go a long way toward easing your concerns and raising your comfort level with technology.

You might ask if online teaching is easier than teaching in the traditional lecture format. To put it bluntly, no. In fact, it can be argued that it is more difficult and time consuming. If you start embracing asynchronous, remote teaching, there is an attendant obligation to make yourself readily accessible beyond the parameters of class time or office hours. Consider, for example, online tests. In a traditional lecture class, the test would be administered during the allotted class time and then graded and returned according to the instructor's schedule. The teacher's time commitment is limited to test development, administration of the test, and grading. Test development is a straightforward process driven by course content. Test administration is generally constrained to the allocated class time. There are several ways to approach grading. The quickest method is using impersonal Scantron bubble sheets, which makes grading a simple matter of filling out an answer key for scanning and grading. Tests that are hand graded will take more time than bubble sheets, but again are fairly easily accomplished or even delegated. Essentially, once established, the time commitment for a test of this nature is fairly stable.

By comparison, the time requirements for developing an online test are similar; however, since I do not secure my tests, students can easily copy the questions. This means I have to revise my tests every semester, which requires a much larger bank of test questions. There are ways to secure online tests, thus protecting the question bank. But since my approach is to allow students the opportunity to use the tests as a study resource, I haven't pursued that option. I willingly accept the additional time requirements to make the course more user friendly. When it comes down to test administration, the online test requires less time than the traditional testing method, because all I have to do is establish release criteria, such as dates, submission options, time restrictions, and so forth. This takes about five minutes, after which administration of the test is on autopilot and is the responsibility of the student.

Tests are released for a week, during which time students are allowed one chance to take them; once they begin they must continue until time runs out or until they formally submit the test, whichever comes first. Upon submission, students can review their test and see their performance on specific questions. For some questions, the program automatically provides feedback based upon their chosen response. Eventually, I hope to have all questions configured with this feedback option. Despite the time-consuming nature of adding this option, I believe it is worthwhile, as it provides a mechanism to give students valuable and timely feedback. Once the test has closed, I blend students' online efforts back into class by using the learning management system's item analysis feature, which provides specific statistical information on students' response pattern for each question. For example, take a multiple-choice question with a correct response of *b*. If 85% of the class gets this question correct, then it is safe to assume the question is well written and reflective of covered content. However, if only 60% of the class answered correctly, and the remaining 40% were distributed more or less evenly between responses *a*, *c*, and *d*, then you may have a problem with the way the question or responses are worded, or with how you covered the related content. Either way, a problem exists. Use of the item analysis feature helps isolate questions with problems, which I bring back to the face-to-face forum for discussion and clarification.

Keeping computer limitations in mind, students may see they lost points for errors such as misspellings, omitting a hyphen in a spelled-out number, or perhaps for making a response plural instead of singular. Scantron bubble sheets do not have these problems, and teachers automatically compensate when hand grading, but without specific programming, computers cannot. So, in fairness to the students, I review the course site and adjust tests daily, even periodically checking it at nights and on weekends, just in case students have access issues or technology questions. This time commitment exceeds that associated with grading a traditional test; however, I prefer this method because it gives me the ability to offer specific feedback, clarification, and guidance wherever needed, something that would be more difficult with bubble sheet tests. In practice, most technological issues that occur are quickly and easily resolved. My point is that asynchronous, remote learning does not mean relinquishing teaching responsibilities to the computer. Online teaching has benefits for the students as much as or more than it does for the instructor, such as in the case of nontraditional students who might be older, career changers, employed full- or part-time, or married with families and all the attendant commitments. For these students, completing even a part of their course work at home and at their discretion while still having remote access to the instructor can make a big difference.

Remote asynchronous access was one of the driving reasons I designed another course, HTM 398: Cuisine and Culture, in a blended learning fashion. Every year I lead a spring break study-abroad program in a different part of Europe to provide students with firsthand culinary and cultural experiences. Since this is only an eight-day journey, I schedule on-campus lectures during the semester to increase my students' exposure to the topics for the trip. The class meets biweekly prior to leaving. Topics covered include regional history and culinary traditions, while more specific topics include food tastings, basic language lessons, and issues related to traveling. Students are assigned presentations regarding the specific itinerary, such as site visits, food production methods, and cultural traditions, with the goal of becoming the content expert or tour guide once we actually visit the site or experience the tradition in question.

In the online component, course readings and assignments are posted on the learning management system's course site and scheduled for release in a timed fashion that complements the lecture. For example, a previous program focused on Switzerland with a tour that began in Zurich and ended in Lausanne. During this journey, the culinary component included a praline and pastry factory, cheese museum, winery, microbrewery, glass factory, five-star hotel, chocolate maker, and food museum, while the historical component included guided city tours of Geneva, Bern, and Lucerne, sampling regionally specific meals such as fondue and raclette, and touring historical sites, such as Château de Chillon, a medieval castle on the banks of Lake Geneva.

Prior to the trip, I had a student team present the castle's history in class. The day after their presentation, I posted online a short architectural description of the various parts of a castle and their historical roles, along with several links to reliable resources. Finally, I released an assignment, which consisted of a typical castle diagram with blanks for the students to complete. After listening to their peers' lecture, reading the posted article, and completing the online assignment, the students were prepared for their visit to the castle. They were able to identify its various elements such as the parapet, bailey, curtain wall, and barbican. They had cultivated an appreciation for the time and effort that went into the castle's construction, and an understanding of its history and historical role in the region. Lesson content was delivered in multiple ways and finally blended in a tangible face-to-face encounter.

In another example, student teams gave presentations on the art of cheese making, sampled different cheeses in class, read a posted essay about the food science involved in making cheese, downloaded a customized crossword puzzle assignment, and while in Switzerland, toured the museum factory and sampled real Gruyère cheese. The same blended learning approach was used with the topics of chocolate, beer, and wine making; content was introduced face-to-face, emphasized with online components, and then reinforced through a real-world, hands-on travel experience. For this class, online assignments, readings, and exams related to student presentations and the journey created an integrated blended learning approach, and since we only met every other week, the online course site, with its asynchronous remote capabilities, kept the class moving forward in a seamless fashion with course resources, calendar prompts, pop-up notices, and communication tools.

I choose to use blended learning methods in my classroom for several reasons, none of which have much to do with saving time or labor. The primary reason is because it allows me to teach from multiple perspectives. Online technology permits me to connect with the students individually through e-mail, in small groups through the group manager, or with the whole class through discussion threads, chat rooms, and e-mail. Streaming videos, tutorials, and slide shows offer students the ability to reinforce lecture content at their convenience. Content learned in an online format, such as assignments and tests, is woven through the lecture, which allows me to expand students' understanding.

The face-to-face lectures allow for spontaneity and provide a platform for practical demonstrations and tastings, without which one could not develop a true understanding of culinary ingredients or cooking methods. For example, during the course component addressing seasoning and flavoring, students have online access to the lecture notes and a supplemental slide-show presentation illustrating the most common herbs and seasonings, proper storage procedures, and specific preparation issues. Then during class I bring in examples of some unique herbs and spices and pass them around the class for students to smell and taste. Seasoning and flavoring is an important culinary skill that simply can't be fully appreciated in an online environment. It is always interesting to have students taste an herb or spice in an isolated context, where they get the full impact of its flavor. Inevitably, a conversation begins, and the lecture expands to encompass students' personal perceptions of taste and of foods they have eaten. Spontaneous discussions of this nature engage students by making the material personally relevant.

Although not quite as spontaneous, another example is the Restaurants and Nutrition assignment. During the face-to-face component, I begin with a presentation showing pictures of common restaurant meals and dishes. I then point out the nutritional value of each dish. Once the students realize that the typical Mexican combo plate comes with a nutritional price tag of 1,184 calories and more than 62 grams of fat, I have their attention. They begin talking and questioning the nutritional values of their favorite meals and menus. At this point the students are fully engaged, so the next step is to bring up the topic of restaurant responsibility and liability, the real scope of the assignment. Being a somewhat sensational and provocative topic, this assignment never fails to encourage a vigorous debate. You might call it *cultivated spontaneity*, in that the stage is set, but the script not fully written. It may seem as if most of the learning occurs in the face-to-face experience; however, I truly believe that the online component provides the groundwork that levels the playing field and promotes the confidence students need to participate. I doubt the debate would be as rich, or the students as engaged, without the preliminary online work.

Finally, I like the way the online components expand the course beyond the scope of the classroom. If I were to administer the tests in class, it would be at the expense of five days' worth of additional content, since students are given 75 minutes to take each test. With the tests, the students are given the responsibility for acquiring the fundamental knowledge outside class so that they are better prepared to engage in the subsequent lecture activity. However, the online content is user friendly in that students choose the when, where, and how of their participation, based upon clearly established criteria. These are the reasons that led me to embrace blended learning; you will notice that convenience is not listed.

Interestingly enough, the more I blend my HTM 291: Quantity Food Production course, the greater the spread I seem to see in the course grades. While this may seem backward, I think it simply reflects a more accurate assessment of student performance. Remember, when I first began teaching, my students were not purchasing the textbook because I was spoon-feeding them the course material. They didn't have to think; basic memorization was all I demanded from them. In that scenario, it was difficult *not* to get an A. Now, with clearly defined rules and roles, they are forced to assume some of the responsibility for their education. Consequently, there is more variation in course grades; about a third of the class will earn an A, while the rest are divided between Bs and Cs and even the occasional D or F. You might think this would result in student complaints, but course evaluations for the most part reflect increased satisfaction scores and positive comments about the flexible nature of the course, especially the online components. I have never had a student attribute his or her lack of performance to any of the online features.

One final word. Imagine a pendulum. At one extreme, we find face-to-face educational techniques, such as lectures and demonstrations—traditional methods that have stood the test of time but with certain limitations. At the other extreme, we find modern technological approaches, such as computer-based and online learning—exciting methods full of promise and potential but, again, with limitations. Somewhere in the middle lies blended learning, a method that when properly employed leverages the best of both worlds. From my perspective as a chef and instructor, blended learning has definite applications in culinary arts education. My students are still a tough audience, but today I feel they are engaged and motivated and, therefore, learning.

REFERENCES

Bloom, B. S. E., Engelhart, M. D., Furst, E. J., Hill, W. H., & Krathwohl, D. R. (1956). *Taxonomy of educational objectives: The classification of educational goals. Handbook 1: Cognitive domain* (1st ed.). New York, NY: David McKay.

Chen, C., & Jones, K. (2007). Blended learning vs. traditional classroom settings: Assessing effectiveness and student perceptions in an MBA accounting course. *Journal of Educators Online, 4*(1). Retrieved from http://www.thejeo.com/Vol ume4Number1/JonesFinal.pdf

Garrison, D. R., & Kanuka, H. (2004). Blended learning: Uncovering its transformative potential in higher education. *The Internet and Higher Education, 7*(2), 95–105.

Keller, J. M. (1999). Using the ARCS motivational process in computer-based instruction and distance education. *New Directions for Teaching and Learning,* (78), 39–47.

Krathwohl, D. R. (2002). A revision of Bloom's taxonomy: An overview. *Theory Into Practice, 41*(4), 212–218.

Mortera-Gutiérrez, F. (2006). Faculty best practices using blended learning in e-learning and face-to-face instruction. *International Journal on E-Learning, 5*(3), 313.

Osguthorpe, R. T., & Graham, C. R. (2003). Blended learning environments. *Quarterly Review of Distance Education, 4*(3), 227–233.

Phillips, D. C. (1995). The good, the bad, and the ugly: The many faces of constructivism. *Educational Researcher, 24*(7), 5–12.

Thorpe, M. (2002). Rethinking learner support: The challenge of collaborative online learning. *Open Learning, 17*, 105–119.

2

Baby Steps to Blended

Introduction of a Blended Unit to a Conventional Course

Francine S. Glazer

When it comes to course innovations, there are two schools of thought: Jump in headfirst, or take baby steps. What I describe in this chapter is a baby step toward blended in which I developed one unit of a web-enhanced course in a blended format. I describe the thought process that went into developing the unit and discuss implementation hurdles, how it improved student learning, students' reactions, and subsequent revisions.

Principles of Genetics is not a typical gateway course, since it is generally not taken in the freshman year, nor is it one of the first courses in the biology major. Even so, it frequently causes students much more difficulty than do other courses. Generally taken in the second or third year, the emphasis on logic and data analysis demanded by classical genetics creates a hurdle for many students.

SO MUCH INFORMATION, SO LITTLE TIME

To exacerbate the problem, the course, like many courses in many disciplines, simply tries to do too much. General biology programs often include only one semester of genetics, and that course often introduces three very different subdisciplines: classical (or organismal) genetics, population genetics, and molecular genetics. Molecular genetics alone could easily take one semester, so the course overflows with content. Unfortunately, the overflow phenomenon extends to the students, who find it difficult to absorb and structure so much new information.

Faced with the dilemma of how to introduce students to the three different branches of genetics while preserving time for students to actually think and solve problems in class, I transformed the course from a traditional

31

lecture format into a team-based learning course, after the model of Michaelson, Knight, and Fink (2004).

Team-based learning is a highly structured form of cooperative learning (Johnson, Johnson, & Smith, 1991; Millis, 2010; Millis & Cottell, 1997). Students are grouped into permanent teams for the semester and work on sophisticated problems and applications. A unit begins with students preparing at home (yes, really!), using a reading guide provided by the professor. The first item on the classroom agenda is a concept-level quiz that students take individually and then as a team. Next comes an appeals process in which teams can present a written appeal to answers marked incorrect on the team quiz. At that point, students have a good working knowledge of the content, so the real work can begin. The majority of class time is spent solving problems and working on complex applications of the material.

Team-based learning worked beautifully for the genetics course. For example, students come to class with a working knowledge of the terminology and even of Mendel's first and second laws, and are able to do basic monohybrid crosses (i.e., predict the offspring of two individuals who differ in only one trait). The quizzes and appeals process provides an opportunity to clarify areas of confusion, which means we can spend our time together working on more complex applications of Mendel's laws, such as three-point crosses (i.e., a procedure used to determine the sequence of genes on a chromosome). I found that the students were able to discuss, absorb, and use more information more skillfully. And better yet, students were not only passing the course, they were enjoying it.

Even with these improvements, I was struggling with ways to improve the molecular genetics portion of the course. Students were getting lost in the minutiae and needed an organizing strategy. My decision to use a case study served two purposes: It provided an organizing framework for the information and added another dimension to the team-based learning design of the course by providing a complex, ill-structured, collaborative task.

CONSTRUCTING THE CASE STUDY

Case studies help students deal with abstract material by providing a story line that makes the material more tangible (Boehrer & Linsky, 1990; Gallucci, 2006; Herreid, 1994, 2004, 2005; Styer, 2009). I needed to create a story that would make them want to talk—and learn—about molecular genetics, with components that could be tackled online and others that would benefit from the synergy of the classroom. Genetically modified organisms seemed like an ideal choice, introducing molecular techniques, commercial applications ranging from pharmaceuticals to the food supply, and a host of societal and ethical issues.

Knowing in advance that I wanted to use the case in a blended format, I decided to create a case study (see Appendix A for the case study and Appendix B for the grading rubrics) that could be tackled in stages. With that in mind, I created my story line. The setting is a community garden. The characters are Irene, an organic gardener, and Sunita, a gardener who wanted to introduce recombinant potatoes. The plot is a disagreement that increases in intensity and eventually goes to mediation. The finale is an in-class mediation, with different teams playing different roles: the organic gardener (Irene), the troublemaker who wanted to plant those newfangled potatoes (Sunita), the administrator of the community garden who served as the mediator (Pat), and two expert witnesses—a biotechnologist (Chris) and a bioethicist (Miguel). (As a side note, I named the characters in the story after some of my students from previous years. The students in the current class were entertained to see the names of their friends and occasionally, their tutors, and it seemed to increase their engagement even more.)

Layering the Activity

As I worked on the details of the case study, I had to consider which elements would best lend themselves to the built-in opportunities for reflection that occur online, and which would best lend themselves to the spontaneity that occurs face-to-face. An interesting dynamic in this creative process is trying to create a case study with questions and activities that are pedagogically sound, and trying to create activities that make best use of the in- and out-of-class opportunities. I found that I flipped back and forth between the two mind-sets, first working on one and then the other. I felt a bit like a sailboat tacking against the wind, going in two different directions as I tried to get to a place in between. I do the same here, briefly summarizing the case study and then discussing how its structure might change in a wholly face-to-face setting as opposed to how it functions in the blended environment it was designed for.

Ultimately, the finished case study had three stages, or sections. Part 1 was very brief, serving to introduce the characters and the concept of a community garden, and to ensure everyone was using a common definition of the term *organic* as it applied to food. Part 2 extended the conversation about organic versus recombinant organisms, supplying ample points of entry to the content for further investigation. By the end of Part 2, the two characters reached an impasse and decided to go for mediation to resolve their conflict. Part 3 sets the stage for the mediation itself.

Had the case been conducted entirely face-to-face, I would have combined Parts 1 and 2. In the face-to-face class students would read the first parts (1 and 2) of the case study in class and then discuss them, answering the questions they knew and developing a research strategy for the remaining questions. After out-of-class time during which students did individual research, more class time would be allotted for students to strategize how to prepare for the mediation event. Especially given the constraints of a commuter campus, it would perhaps have been necessary to stretch the preparation time to an additional week and include small chunks of class time for the teams to regroup prior to the mediation.

However, in a blended environment, I wanted to leverage the students' ability to meet asynchronously in their groups as a way of deepening their engagement with the material. The short straightforward Part 1 allowed me to briefly introduce the case study in class. Student teams could do some initial work face-to-face and get a sense of each other prior to taking on the more complex Part 2 and dividing it up to research. Part 2, therefore, took place entirely online in private discussion forums.

Evolution of a Blended Activity

The case study was my first attempt to deliberately blend an aspect of the course, although other aspects of the course had begun blending organically, originating with student activity. I began using a course management system to house the materials for the course so students could access them at any time. I'd also set up some discussion boards for students to ask questions about the material as they studied at home, and the discussions were becoming popular. When students in teams started using the discussions to arrange times and places to meet—always a challenge for a commuter campus—I set up discussion forums for each group so they could work together.

The group forums proved serendipitous. Watching the students use them to communicate, I realized they were spending additional time on the course. Students were coming to class better prepared and more excited. They were more conversant with the material, which meant that the students often integrated more concepts than they had previously in the in-class discussions. Creating the case study as a blended activity capitalized on this growing momentum, facilitating student collaboration and increasing time on task.

Chickering and Gamson (1987) identified time on task as one of the seven principles for good practice in undergraduate education, saying, "Time plus energy equals learning." Chickering and Ehrmann (1996) expanded on this principle as it applies to technology, pointing out that online availability of resources can increase available time by decreasing commuting time. My working hypothesis, then, was that implementing the case study as a blended module, rather than strictly face-to-face, would improve the quality of student work by increasing the amount of time students spent on task as well as their access to and use of online resources.

Role Play

Part 3 sets the stage for the mediation. I chose to introduce Part 3, including what would happen during the mediation, in the face-to-face classroom for two reasons. First, I anticipated a number of questions about how the mediation would be structured. Since it was essential that students understand what they were preparing for, it was simpler and faster to answer these questions as a conversation in the classroom. Second, I had not assigned roles to the teams. I wanted to turn what could be a perfunctory event—choosing roles—into part of the learning process.

Choosing roles for the mediation is a good example of an activity that benefits from the immediacy of face-to-face contact. As I mentioned earlier, there were five student groups and five roles. Rather than simply drawing team names out of a hat and asking each team which character it wanted to play, I wanted each team to seriously consider each one of the five roles before making a choice. In doing so, the teams would have to explore all four areas: the benefits of organic gardening, the benefits of using molecular biology to alter food crops, the molecular genetics techniques required to make those alterations, and the ethical implications of using the technology and the products of that technology.

After Part 3 was distributed to the students, they outlined what they anticipated each character's expertise and position would be. We then had a class discussion about the five characters. In addition to a debriefing on the expertise and position of each character, we also explored as a class the areas of research that might be necessary to prepare for that role. Teams then had five minutes to agree on first, second, and third choices. Names were drawn from a hat to establish the order in which they picked their identities. I deliberately asked them to identify three choices, anticipating that the last team(s) might not get its first or even second choice. The process of selecting three choices helped the teams invest in several characters, which made it easier for them to adapt if they did not get their first choice.

Preparation for the mediation involved researching the topic and preparing a set of talking points, which then became the written record of their work. All this work was conducted online in private discussion forums. I told the students I would lurk in their team's discussion forums, reading everything, but only joining the discussion if I was asked a direct question or if the team needed redirection in a particular area.

The next face-to-face portion of this case was the mediation. Despite lurking in each group's discussion forum and knowing the extent of their preparations, I was quite unprepared for the level of excitement that pervaded the classroom on the day of the mediation. The teams came in with posters, handouts, and presentations. As the mediation moved through different content areas, different members of each team rotated into the dialogue to represent the team's character. The conversation was informed, animated, and purposeful. Best of all, when class ended the students refused to leave, saying things like "We haven't talked through everything that we've prepared," and "We still have arguments to make," until I agreed that we could continue the mediation discussion in the next class meeting.

Because this case is open-ended, each time I've used it, the mediator team has come up with a different decision. The decisions have sometimes been well-supported by the information presented by the various teams and have always been controversial, and the excitement in the class was palpable. In one class, students were so engaged in the case study that the team losing the mediation went so far as to request the opportunity to appeal the decision.

Student Reactions

A reflective essay from the students was a wellspring of useful information. Students wrote that they learned more of the biology and became more interested in it. According to one student, in part, this was because of the case study format: "I think that the case study allowed us to explore information that we are faced with daily but never think about." According to another, in part, it was because of the structure of the activity: "We weren't doing the usual looking in the book and taking an exam kind of deal. Assignments like this teach me more, and interactions with my peers help me to better understand the material."

In particular, the blended format garnered praise. Contributions made by each team member were visible and documented in the discussion forums. If a member did not post his or her work, it was evident. Students appreciated the accountability imposed on all members of the team, as indicated in the following comment:

> I feel that for the most part my group worked extremely well together throughout the preparation process. As soon as the case study was introduced in class, we decided who would work on each question. Then we set deadlines for posting our materials so we could all respond and give feedback or ask questions. . . . I think we all answered our assigned questions clearly and in detail, and it was faster (and more interesting) than having everyone answer all the questions themselves.

Lessons Learned: Timing of Activities

One thing I learned from the student response papers was the importance of the timeline. If there was too much time between online and in-class activities, continuity was lost; if there was not enough, students came into class without the necessary knowledge. Many students completed their posts so close to class time that significant numbers of students replicated the work on their own or came to class frustrated that they did not have the information to proceed to the next stage. One student commented,

> Sometimes team members posted information late, or it was incomplete. Then the rest of us had to research their questions if we wanted to be prepared for class, and there wasn't much time to get it done. If the due dates were earlier, 2 or 3 days before class, then posts would be up early enough for all of us to discuss. That way if something wasn't clear, we would have sufficient time to do deeper research in order to understand the concepts.

This issue caught me by surprise. I'd taught fully online courses before and had what I thought was a good understanding of how to pace an asynchronous discussion. If anything, I thought the in-class sessions would help keep students on track. What I hadn't anticipated was the need to explicitly allow for reading and thinking time. A number of students posted their contributions so close to the start of class that their teammates did not have enough time to process the information or ask for elaboration. If blending is to be successful, it's not enough to intertwine online and in-class components; there also has to be a third strand—time to think.

In his book, *Creating Significant Learning Experiences*, Dee Fink (2003) proposes structuring the learning activities for a course so that in-class activities alternate with out-of-class activity (see Figure 2.1).

Figure 2.1   The "Castle Top" Diagram: A General Template for Creating a Teaching Strategy

In-class:	Active Learning / Student Interactions		Active Learning / Student Interactions		Active Learning / Student Interactions		Exam
Out-of-class:		Read text		Homework exercises		Review	

Note. Adapted from *Creating Significant Learning Experiences: An Integrated Approach to Designing College Courses,* by L. D. Fink, 2003, San Francisco, CA: Jossey-Bass, p. 132. Copyright 2003 by Jossey-Bass. Reproduced with permission of Wiley & Sons, Inc.

At first blush, this structure seems ideally designed for blended courses. After all, don't blended courses by definition meld in-class and out-of-class activities? What I learned from my students, though, suggests the need for a third tier in the diagram, so that there are strands for in-class, blended, and out-of-class time (see Figure 2.2). Students need to interact online and also need time to reflect on what they've learned and put it into context with the rest of the material in order to proceed.

Lessons Learned: Mediation Session

As a culminating activity, the mediation session was a great success, if somewhat disorganized and short on time. Students came away from the mediation able to express the views of all the characters in the case study despite

Figure 2.2   The "Castle Top" Diagram Adapted for a Blended Learning Course

In-class:	Active Learning / Student Interactions		Active Learning / Student Interactions		Active Learning / Student Interactions		Exam
BL:	Active Learning / Student Interactions / Reflection		Active Learning / Student Interactions / Reflection		Active Learning / Student Interactions / Reflection		Authentic Assessment
Out-of-class:		Read text		Homework exercises		Review	

Note. This modification of Fink's model illustrates the third type of time that exists in blended courses.

having only prepared to represent a single point of view. Additionally, students finished the mediation with clear, well-supported personal opinions: "I now have a broader view of genetically modified organisms and the varying views on the topic."

Students provided some invaluable suggestions regarding the mediation. As with the preparation phase of the case study, time was also an issue. The students wanted more time for the mediation than just one class period so they would have more time to reflect on and absorb the information. One student suggested that we "leave Pat's [the mediator's] ruling until the next class and allow a day to post the characters' main points on Blackboard for other groups to read before Pat makes a decision."

Students also expressed loud and clear the need for better organization. Several students suggested a debate format, with Pat asking questions of each participant, to allow everyone a chance to speak and to enable students to organize the information in their mind as they learned it. A related suggestion was to allow each group to make brief opening and concluding statements so they had the opportunity to present a coherent case:

> We put so much time into preparations, and it was frustrating not to have enough time to make our points. It would have been helpful to me if there had been time for each team to introduce themselves and their points of view at the beginning of the mediation, and to have each team give a brief recap at the conclusion. Plus, if Pat didn't make a decision until the next class, we could all post our talking points online for everyone else to read.

In view of student comments, I've made some changes to the mediation in preparation for offering this unit again. First and foremost, students clearly wanted more time. They had prepared extensively and did not feel they had enough time to make their points and demonstrate their knowledge. Second, they wanted more structure. It seemed that Pat, the mediator, did not have control over the conversation's flow, as illustrated by the two following comments:

> This was the first time I was actually in a class debate in which I had to participate and it still seems that I wasn't able to put in two cents.

> Pat needed to maintain better control over the discussion.

Pat needs more intensive preparation—including some additional resources to use for guidance—in effective mediation, and more time to reflect to make a thoughtful and well-supported decision. Even the team who portrayed Pat agreed that Pat did not really have control of the session:

> Although short, the Gardening in Eden Mediation Session was one of the best in-class discussions I have ever participated in; I just wish our team did a better job of mediating.

In my revised version, the mediation will span two class periods. The first day will start with five-minute opening statements from Irene, Sunita, Chris, and Miguel. Five minutes is not enough time for them to spill out all their information but should be enough to state their position and highlight some of the supporting arguments. During the discussion that follows, all the participants must be recognized by Pat in order to speak.

At the end of the first class, the mediation will go into recess. Before the next class meeting, all the groups will have to evaluate what they've presented and how well they've communicated their positions. They can regroup and determine what points they need to make most strongly at the next meeting. Similarly, Pat will evaluate the information presented and make a preliminary decision, creating a written statement that explains the rationale. Pat will also be required to prepare a list of specific questions for each participant to elucidate information that may support or challenge the preliminary decision.

The second part of the mediation will be driven by Pat's questions. Each participant will have five minutes to make a closing statement, arguing his or her case, and if necessary rebutting other points. Pat will then revisit the preliminary decision and make any necessary revisions before presenting it to the class.

I anticipate that extending the mediation to a second class period will result in even deeper learning by the students. They will have time to process what happened in the first session, analyze their arguments in the context of those presented by the other teams, and refine their presentations accordingly.

Lessons Learned: Time Management and Student Expectations

When I talk about blended learning with my colleagues, often the conversation turns to time management. Faculty don't want to feel constantly on call and they worry that a blended course will consume every spare moment. My own experiences in terms of time spent are positive, as a result of two simple strategies that I put into place in the beginning.

First, I told the students—online and in the course syllabus—how frequently and at what times of day they could expect me to log into the course management system.

A simple chart, illustrated in Figure 2.3, indicates whether I log in morning, midday, or early evening. When they post a question students know how long it would reasonably be until I responded.

Second, I directed all questions about assignments to the discussion board. I created a forum called Instructor's Office for that purpose and made sure the students knew that the first thing I did upon logging into the course management system was read and respond to any questions posted there. If someone e-mailed me a question, I posted the question on the Instructor's Office forum, answered it there, and replied to the student's e-mail with a brief, "Great question! I posted the question and my response on the Instructor's Office forum so everyone else could see it, too. Please check there for my response and use the Instructor's Office forum for any follow-up questions you might have." I only had to do this once or twice, and then the students caught on.

The students and I found this method to be a time saver. Sometimes their questions had already been asked and answered. If not, students could ask their questions without waiting until the next class meeting, and everyone saw the same reply, which removed any ambiguity because of selective hearing. Because the students knew when to expect a reply, they didn't have to waste time logging in just to check.

The blended approach also meant that we didn't need to use class time for progress updates—I could simply look at the group forums. I was able to

Figure 2.3 Instructor Availability

I log into the course six days a week. I do not log in from midafternoon Friday through Sunday morning. While exact times vary, I try to log in at least twice each day the rest of the week. Here is an approximate schedule:

Day	Morning	Midday	Evening
Sunday	X		X
Monday	X	X	
Tuesday	X		X
Wednesday	X	X	
Thursday	X		X
Friday	X	X	
Saturday			

monitor groups' private discussions as well, which enabled me to see who was contributing and how well they worked together, and to answer questions that arose in the context of their group work.

In terms of time spent in preparation, again, I think it was comparable. I would have needed to prepare the written materials regardless of whether they were used in the classroom or online, so the only additional document preparation was the instructions for the talking points and mediation. I suspect I would have spent at least as much time clarifying the process in a class discussion as I did in preparing the written document.

LOOKING AHEAD

Will I run this activity again? Yes, definitely. My students were engaged, excited, enthusiastic. Students found and incorporated additional resources into their work. Based on the extent of the discussions and the quality of the talking points, they put more time and effort into preparing for this part of the course than they did for the other, nonblended, parts. Discussion during the mediation was intense and animated, and student comments revealed a degree of critical thinking and analysis that I don't often see in such a content-heavy course.

Will I convert the entire course to a blended format? I hope so. It will require a considerable investment of time up front in rethinking what I do. Instead of a highly interactive lecture-turned-discussion that evolves intuitively in the classroom, I'd have to think back to what the points were that stimulated those conversations and use them to develop questions and activities that could yield a satisfying asynchronous discussion.

More daunting to me personally, though, will be the development of learning objects analogous to those used by Tracey Gau in her World Literature course described in Chapter 4. I had previously been skeptical of the value of learning objects, but after working with her I see their potential. They allow students to organize information and to self-assess, but more importantly they help the students create a visual framework for the massive amount of information they are learning. In a course like genetics, such a framework is invaluable.

As I think about a fully blended version of my genetics course, what I see is the following: a course that front loads information by putting it online, using a combination of reading, online discussion, and interactive learning objects to help students grasp the basic concepts. In class we take that foundational knowledge and the basic concepts and build on them.

Team-based learning will undoubtedly remain part of the course structure too, since the subject lends itself so well to complex problems that have multiple solutions. Activities such as this case study are ideal ways to encourage integration of content learned in genetics with content learned in other biology courses and in other disciplines.

Can I do this all at once? Probably not. The creation of the multimedia— indeed, the conceptualization of what it needs to do—will take awhile. What I do know is that I will keep taking baby steps and see where they take me.

REFERENCES

Boehrer, J., and M. Linsky. (1990). Teaching with cases: Learning to question. *New Directions for Teaching and Learning*, (42), 41–57.

Chickering, A. W., & Ehrmann, S. C. (1996). Implementing the seven principles: Technology as lever. *AAHE Bulletin, 49*(2), 3–6.

Chickering, A. W., & Gamson, Z. (1987). Seven principles for good practice in undergraduate education. *AAHE Bulletin, 40*(7), 3–7.

Fink, L. D. (2003). *Creating significant learning experiences: An integrated approach to designing college courses.* San Francisco, CA: Jossey-Bass.

Gallucci, K. (2006). Learning concepts with cases. *Journal of College Science Teaching, 36*(2), 16–20.

Herreid, C. F. (1994). Case studies in science: A novel method of science education. *Journal of College Science Teaching, 23*, 221–229.

Herreid, C. F. (2004). Can case studies be used to teach critical thinking? *Journal of College Science Teaching, 33*(6), 12–14.

Herreid, C. F. (2005). The interrupted case method. *Journal of College Science Teaching, 35*(2), 4–5.

Johnson, D. J., Johnson, R., & Smith, K. J. (1991). *Active learning: Cooperation in the college classroom.* Edina, MN: Interaction.

Michaelson, L. K., Knight, A., & Fink, D. (Eds.). (2004). *Team-based learning: A transformative use of small groups in college teaching.* Sterling, VA: Stylus.

Millis, B. J. (Ed.). (2010). *Cooperative learning in higher education: Across the disciplines, across the academy.* Sterling, VA: Stylus.

Millis, B. J., & Cottell, P. G., Jr. (1997). *Cooperative learning for higher education faculty.* Phoenix, AZ: Oryx Press.

Styer, S. C. (2009). Constructing and using case studies in genetics to engage students in active learning. *American Biology Teacher, 71*(3), 142–143.

Appendix A: The Case Study
Gardening in Eden

PART 1: INTRODUCTIONS (IN CLASS)

It was a beautiful sunny day, unusual for mid-March. Irene had decided to take advantage of it by turning over her garden patch in the community gardens, getting a jump on spring planting. She was enjoying the birds and the sunshine when she noticed a young woman coming up the path.

"Hello. Can you tell me where area 32 is?" the young woman inquired.

"Right here, next to mine. I have number 31," replied Irene. "Have you taken it to plant?"

"Yes. I'm Sunita," replied the young woman. "I've just signed up in the office now, and thought I'd come take a look."

"Wonderful! I'm Irene. That patch has been unplanted for a couple of years now; it'll be nice to have a neighbor." The two women shook hands and continued to chat as Sunita wandered around area 32, pulling up the occasional weed.

"What do you do?" asked Irene.

"I'm a molecular biologist over at MCP Biotech. You?"

"I work at Sutton, Lindsley, and Price. I'm an accountant. Gardening lets me do something that doesn't involve a calculator," Irene smiled.

"How long have you been planting here?" asked Sunita.

"Fourteen years, ever since they opened," replied Irene. "I can't imagine not growing my own veggies any more. Organic vegetables just taste so much better than store bought, don't you think? How about you—are you new to gardening?"

"No, actually I'm a long-timer, too. I've just moved here from St. Louis a few months ago. I had a big garden there, but here I have an apartment with no yard. I was thrilled to find out that the city has these community gardens!"

Sunita and Irene worked in amicable silence for a while, then parted with "Nice to meet you" and "See you soon" ringing in the late afternoon sunlight.

DISCUSSION QUESTIONS

1. What is a community garden?
2. Define *organic* as it is used in this context. Why would someone want to garden organically?

PART 2: COMPLICATIONS (ONLINE IN TEAMS)

April arrived, and Sunita decided to get started planting her seedlings. She gathered up her supplies and headed down to the gardens where she started digging. She was so engrossed in what she was doing that she didn't hear Irene until a cheery "Hello, neighbor!" broke her concentration. Glad for the break, the two women chatted amiably. "What are you planting?" asked Sunita, noticing Irene's flatbed of seedlings.

"Tomatoes, carrots, radishes, and squash today. It's still a little early to put in lettuce. And this section over here," Irene gestured, "will be sweet corn. How 'bout yourself?"

"I'm starting off slowly today," replied Sunita. "Just cucumbers, squash, and potatoes. I figure I'll put in the rest next week—I'm planning for tomatoes, zucchini, eggplant, and peppers."

"Sounds like a great ratatouille!" commented Irene. "You're ambitious, growing potatoes. I've never had the stomach for fighting with the potato beetles myself."

"Oh, it shouldn't be too hard," responded Sunita. "I've bought Green-Leaf potatoes, so I don't expect to have much trouble at all."

"GreenLeaf potatoes? Is that a new variety?"

"Yes. They have the *Bacillus thuringiensis* toxin gene inserted into them, so they make the Bt toxin that kills the potato beetles. I won't have to use any pesticides at all. Isn't that fantastic?!" enthused Sunita.

Irene grew distracted. "I'm familiar with *B. thuringiensis*," she replied. "I spray the live bacteria on my plants to control pests, but I don't do it too often—maybe twice a summer." Lost in thought, she mused to herself, "I wonder what will happen to the beetles if they are exposed to the toxin all the time. Will my bacterial spray still be effective, or will the pests become resistant?"

The two women continued their work in silence.

DISCUSSION QUESTIONS

1. How was the Bt gene moved into the potato?
2. What is the practical difference (to the farmer) between using pesticides, using bacteria that produce a toxin, and using plants that produce the bacterial toxin?
3. What are the nutritional/health implications of the three methods in question 2?
4. What does Irene mean when she wonders if the beetles will become resistant to the Bt toxin in the potatoes? How does this resistance develop?
5. Why would Sunita's use of recombinant Bt-potatoes affect Irene's use of the *B. thuringiensis* bacteria?
6. Does Sunita have other options that would be equally effective to growing recombinant Bt-potatoes?
7. Does Irene have other options that would be as equally effective as spraying *B. thuringiensis* bacteria on her crops while maintaining her standards for organic gardening?

PART 3: MEDIATION (STARTS OFF IN CLASS, CONTINUES ONLINE, FINISHES IN CLASS)

Irene and Sunita have reached an impasse. Irene has asked Sunita not to plant the recombinant Bt potatoes, but Sunita is firm in her desire to do so. The two women brought the issue to the director of the community gardens and have agreed to accept the results of a mediation session. The following individuals are present at the mediation session:

- Pat, director of the community gardens. Pat will moderate the discussion, making sure everyone has a chance to state his or her view and to respond to others' points, and will have the responsibility of making the final decision.
- Irene, the complainant. She has requested that Sunita not plant the Bt potatoes, since they may interfere with organic gardening practices.

- Sunita, the respondent. She maintains that Bt potatoes are safe to plant, will not interfere with anyone else's plantings, are less harmful than using externally applied pesticides, and will not negatively affect the environment.
- Chris, a molecular biologist from a biotechnology firm (not the same company where Sunita works), who has been invited to answer questions pertaining to how the Bt potatoes were generated and their safety.
- Miguel, an ethicist from the local university who specializes in biotechnology.

Preparation Notes

- Each team will need to prepare talking points in advance of the mediation session. Talking points will summarize your position and should indicate which team member is responsible for presenting each portion of the information.
- Pat's talking points will differ from the other groups' in that Pat's preparation will focus on process as much as on content. Because Pat is mediating the discussion, Pat must prepare questions to ensure the discussion stays on track. Pat will also need to anticipate ways to redirect the discussion when it drifts off topic.

Mediation Format (revised as per student suggestions)

1. When you arrive in class, you will see that the room is set up with the chairs in two concentric circles. Each team will choose a starting delegate who sits in the inner circle, while his or her teammates sit in the chairs behind their delegate.
2. The only people who can speak are the people sitting in the inner circle. The inner circle contains more seats than people. If a team member wants to join in the discussion, he or she is welcome to do so by moving into an empty seat in the inner circle, at which point that person becomes the team delegate and the original team member moves back to the outer circle.
3. Everyone is expected to rotate into the circle and contribute meaningfully to the discussion at least once during the discussion. If any delegate remains in the circle for more than 10 minutes, Dr. Glazer will stop the mediation so that someone else from that team can rotate in.

4. At the start of Day 1 of the mediation, Irene and Sunita will each make five-minute presentations stating their positions. Chris and Miguel will then make five-minute presentations highlighting some of the relevant background information that must be considered.

5. The bulk of the mediation session will be structured like a debate, with Pat asking questions of the different parties and allowing time for rebuttal. At the end of class, each team will have three minutes to summarize its position, and the mediation will be tabled until the next class meeting.

Between Class Meetings

1. Pat comes to a preliminary decision and writes questions for the specific parties who will either clarify information that was incomplete or confusing, or Pat will allow participants to present information that challenges Pat's decision.

2. The other groups must review their talking points to see what, if anything, was omitted. They should also review their notes from the first session, determining what points they will need to make to strengthen their own position or rebut that of their opponents.

3. At the start of Day 2 of the mediation session, Pat will ask specific questions of each team. Then each team will have five minutes to give a summation, after which the class will go into recess.

4. During the recess, Pat will make a decision and prepare a brief rationale to present. The other teams will use this time to review their notes and their talking points, doing some preliminary analysis on what they did well and what they could have done more effectively.

5. Finally, the class as a whole will debrief. Pat will make the recommendation, and the other participants will have a chance to respond (in character) to the recommendation.

6. After class, you will each write an individual essay reflecting on this assignment (the case study as well as the mediation). Your reflection should address the following questions:
   - What were the strengths of your group's preparation process?
   - What were the weaknesses of your group's preparation process? If you had this activity to do again, how might you modify your own behavior to mitigate any weaknesses you've identified?
   - In your opinion, how effective was the mediation session as a way to bring together all the various points of view? For example, could you articulate another character's point of view clearly?

Do you feel that you have a grasp of all the different angles on this issue?
- Are you satisfied with Pat's recommendation? Why or why not? If not, what would you recommend instead, and why?

This reflection is due, typewritten, no later than one week after the mediation activity is completed.

Appendix B
Assessment Rubrics

Note: These are the rubrics I used to assess online student work. Students had access to the rubrics all semester, so they knew the criteria.

DISCUSSION QUESTIONS RUBRIC (20 POINTS POSSIBLE)

The discussion questions are critical in this activity because they are where you take the factual knowledge you are learning and apply it to more complex problems and situations. In this way, your knowledge of the subject grows deeper, and you have the opportunity to relate what you have learned to practical situations.

The following rubric will be used to assess your participation in discussion question activities.

Initial Posting (3 points)

____ (3) Well-developed ideas, introduces new ideas, stimulates discussion.
____ (2) Developing ideas, sometimes stimulates discussion.
____ (1) Poorly developed ideas, does not add substance to the discussion.
____ (0) Did not enter the discussion.

Responses (3 points)

____ (3) Responses to classmates' postings are clear, understandable, and specific. Well-developed ideas, introduces new ideas, stimulates discussion.
____ (2) Responses to classmates' postings are clearly worded. Developing ideas, sometimes stimulates discussion.

_____ (1) Responses to classmates' postings are worded in confusing manner; classmates need to ask for clarification of the response. Poorly developed ideas, does not add substance to the discussion.

_____ (0) Did not enter the discussion.

Evidence of Critical Thinking (5 points)

_____ (4–5) Clear evidence of critical thinking (application, analysis, synthesis, and evaluation). Postings are characterized by clarity of argument, depth of insight into theoretical issues, originality of treatment, relevancy, and sometimes include unusual insights and flashes of brilliance. Arguments are well supported.

_____ (2–3) Beginnings of critical thinking. Postings tend to address peripheral issues. Generally accurate, but could be improved with more analysis and creative thought. Tendency to recite fact rather than address issues.

_____ (1) Poorly developed critical thinking.

_____ (0) Did not enter the discussion.

Sufficient Number of Interactions (3 points)

_____ (3) Answered assigned question and posted a minimum of two substantive responses to classmates.

_____ (2) Answered assigned question and posted one substantive response.

_____ (1) Posted either answer to assigned question or substantive responses but not both.

_____ (0) Did not enter the discussion.

Mechanics (3 points)

_____ (3) No spelling or grammatical errors, evidencing proofreading, and the meaning of the sentences is clear.

_____ (2) Small number (< 4) of spelling or grammatical errors, but the meaning of the sentences is still understandable.

_____ (1) Large number (> 4) of spelling or grammatical errors; it may be difficult to understand the meaning of some sentences because of poor syntax.

_____ (0) Large number (> 4) of spelling or grammatical errors; many sentences are so poorly written it is difficult to understand the intent of the post.

Timeliness of Initial Postings and Responses (3 points)

____ (3) All postings were made before their respective deadlines.

____ (2) Some items were posted on time; some items were posted after the deadline.

____ (1) All items were posted after the deadline.

____ (0) Did not enter the discussion.

TALKING POINTS RUBRIC (33 POINTS POSSIBLE)

The following rubric will be used to assess your participation in the team project activity. In addition, you will complete the Team Project Self-Evaluation Rubric and send me your self-assessment via the course e-mail.

Content (8 points)

____ (7–8) Both sides of the issue are fairly presented. Information provided is relevant, accurate, and necessary to the scope of the project. Recommendation is clearly stated, and is supported with solidly researched, properly cited information.

____ (5–6) Some bias evident in selection of what materials to include/ exclude, i.e., both sides of the issue are not represented equally well. Information provided is relevant and accurate, but not complete. Recommendation is clearly stated and is supported with evidence.

____ (3–4) Only one side of the issue has been researched and represented in the final product. Recommendation is clearly stated and supported with evidence. Not all sources are reliable.

____ (1–2) Recommendation is present but with little or no supporting research. Sources are not present or not reliable.

____ (0) Some information is presented but no clear recommendation. Little or no research to support recommendation (if present).

Evidence of Critical Thinking (8 points)

____ (7–8) Project demonstrates a high degree of critical thinking and the ability to apply concepts in a practical manner. Paper is a thoughtful analysis of the information rather than a simple description of the information. Information is expressed clearly, and there is a logical flow to ideas. Recommendation is clearly supported by research and analysis of relevant information.

____ (5–6) Project demonstrates critical thinking and the ability to apply concepts.

____ (3–4) Project demonstrates some critical thinking and application of concepts.

____ (1–2) Project shows little demonstration of critical thinking but shows some application of concepts.

____ (0) Project shows minor or incorrect application of concepts.

Collaboration With Team (5 points)

____ (5) Members of the team initiated and maintained exceptional constructive communication in order to complete the assignment. Team members work as a team (not individuals splitting up the assignment), practice consensus building, and all members actively participate in team discussion and project creation. The product created is creative and exceptional.

____ (4) Members of the team initiated and maintained reasonable and constructive communication to complete the assignment. Team members work as a team (not individuals splitting up the assignment), practice consensus building, and most members actively participate in team discussion and project creation. The product created is creative and well done.

____ (3) Team members work as a team by splitting up the assignment, making decisions in regard to achieving the goals as a team, and most members participate in the team discussion and product creation. The product created is adequate.

____ (2) Members work primarily as individuals by splitting up the assignment, making individual decisions in regard to achieving the goals, show little cohesiveness to the team in any way other than task completion. Only a few members actually provide work for the completed project. The product created is adequate.

____ (1) Little to no demonstration of team identity or cooperation. One person primarily responsible for creation of entire project. The product created is less than adequate.

Written Presentation (7 points)

____ (1 if yes; 0 if no) The team project is attractive and professionally presented.

____ (1 if yes; 0 if no) The team project has a title.

_____ (1 if yes; 0 if no) The team project includes the names of the team members.

_____ (1 if yes; 0 if no) The team project contains few or no misspellings or grammatical errors (evidence of proofreading).

_____ (1 if yes; 0 if no) The team project includes references to outside sources of information that were used to complete the project.

_____ (1 if yes; 0 if no) Citations are formatted correctly (in text and endnotes).

_____ (1 if yes; 0 if no) The team project is well organized and easy to follow.

Mechanics (3 points)

_____ (3) Individual points are well structured, citations are used appropriately, and the meaning of the sentences is clear. Jargon is defined on first use.

_____ (2) Small number (< 4) of spelling or grammatical errors, but the meaning of the sentences is still understandable.

_____ (1) Large number (> 4) of spelling or grammatical errors; it may be difficult to understand the meaning of some sentences because of poor syntax.

_____ (0) Large number (> 4) of spelling or grammatical errors; many sentences are so poorly written it is difficult to understand the intent of the post.

Timeliness of Team Project (2 points)

_____ (2) The talking points were completed before the deadline.

_____ (1) The talking points were completed after the deadline.

_____ (0) No talking points prepared.

TEAM PARTICIPATION SELF-ASSESSMENT RUBRIC (6 POINTS POSSIBLE)

Before you do anything else, please save the file with a new name: *SelfAssess6pt_YourLastName.doc*

Please check the box you feel best represents your behavior in the team during this case study. Then, provide a rationale for your self-assessment (the box will expand as you type). Save your changes, and submit this file to the Self-Assessment Drop Box.

Criteria	Always	Sometimes	Never
I participated actively.			
Rationale:			
I did my share of the work.			
Rationale:			
I did not dominate discussions.			
Rationale:			
I helped the group stay on task.			
Rationale:			
I listened carefully to what others were saying.			
Rationale:			
I was receptive to other points of view.			
Rationale:			

REFLECTIVE ESSAY RUBRIC (16 POINTS POSSIBLE)

Content (8 points)

____ (7–8) The questions are addressed in a thoughtful, substantive manner. Responses are relevant, accurate, and complete. Student has obviously reflected on the process used in Gardening in Eden and has identified strengths and areas that could be improved (questions 1, 2, and 3). Student demonstrates a clear and comprehensive understanding of the content of the case (questions 3 and 4).

____ (5–6) The questions are addressed, but to varying extents; not all responses are thoughtful or complete. Student has identified strengths or weaknesses of the process used in Gardening in Eden. Student has a good understanding of the content of the case.

____ (3–4) All questions are answered, but most or all are answered in a cursory manner. Minimal reflection is evident based on the responses.

____ (1–2) Only some of the questions are answered. Very little if any reflection is evident based on the responses.

____ (0) No useful information is conveyed in the essay.

Evidence of Critical Thinking (4 points)

____ (4) Essay demonstrates a high degree of critical thinking and the ability to apply concepts in a practical manner. Paper is a thoughtful analysis of the process and product rather than a simple description. Information is expressed clearly, and there is a logical flow to ideas.

____ (2–3) Essay demonstrates some critical thinking and the ability to apply concepts.

____ (1) Essay shows little demonstration of critical thinking but shows some application of concepts.

____ (0) Essay shows minor or incorrect application of concepts.

Presentation (4 points)

____ (1 if yes; 0 if no) The essay has a title.

____ (1 if yes; 0 if no) The essay includes the name of the author.

____ (1 if yes; 0 if no) The essay contains few or no misspellings or grammatical errors (evidence of proofreading).

____ (1 if yes; 0 if no) The essay is well organized and easy to follow.

3

Teaching a Survey Course in Anthropology

Alan Aycock

For the past four years, I've taught an anthropology course titled Survey of World Cultures (SWC). I confess that initially I agreed to teach the course somewhat reluctantly (to tell the truth, I had carefully avoided teaching this course for about three decades). I find the notion of a course that professes to survey the cultures of the world more than a little unfocused if not in fact a wholly impossible task.

It was in large part the daunting nature of my teaching assignment that led me initially to examine the pedagogical possibilities and challenges more closely, then to explore different ways to teach the course. I've now taught SWC several times in face-to-face, fully online, and in hybrid or blended mode, so I think I've a better grasp of the pedagogical repertoire for this course than I did when I first began to teach it.

The course itself is an introductory-level offering in cultural anthropology. However, it is not the main introduction to our discipline; instead, SWC is a general education course that enrolls few anthropology majors. The course does, however, attract many students whose programs require an exposure to cultural diversity (e.g., pre-med and business students, criminal justice majors, and undergraduate fine arts students). It finally occurred to me, after fussing over issues such as coverage and assessment, that it was precisely the *absence* of a large contingent of anthropology majors that allowed me greater flexibility in course design and delivery.

The size of the course has steadily grown over the years. It began as a relatively manageable seminar of 30–40 students; it has now more than doubled in enrollment. This has meant, as we shall see, that I've had to reconsider my methods of student assessment to keep the course workload at a reasonable level, and to look for ways to maintain student engagement in an increasingly large classroom.

Students who take this course are—as is the case with most other anthropology courses—about two thirds women. Minority students make up about 10% of the class. The vast majority of the students are first-generation college students from rural, working-class backgrounds. Many of them have experienced very little diversity in their own lives, although I've found that most students are extremely curious about lifestyles other than their own. Thus a pedagogical problem (Bass, 1999), the lack of sophistication or diversity of many of the students enrolled in the course, is balanced by a pedagogical opportunity, the willingness of the students to learn more.

Finally, many of the students have taken courses in which traditional modes of face-to-face instruction dominate: Straight-up lecturing allied with three exams and a term paper is the model of pedagogy my students are most familiar with. This means one of my first tasks is to shape the expectations of my students regarding the kinds of work they will be doing, the advantages of active learning, and the entirely new cadence of course work (i.e., much faster) in a blended course.

I present the process of course redesign in four areas—content; assessment; the development of an active, engaged peer learning community online; and development of an active, engaged peer learning community in the face-to-face classroom—each of which I address in turn. I draw up the threads of my narrative into a greater fabric by working through the process of designing course modules that integrate face-to-face and online learning. I conclude by observing how blended courses represent my commitment to continuing pedagogical experimentation, and suggest some lessons learned during the process so far, as well as future directions I am now considering for SWC.

CONTENT

Content in SWC includes texts or readings, videos, and lectures. To be eligible for inclusion, content has to be intrinsically engaging for students whose reading habits—according to my surveys—tend to be sporadic at best. Videos are especially helpful in this regard, since students in SWC are avid TV watchers. Lectures are a necessary evil in the sense that they represent the authorial presence of the course instructor. It's not clear, though, that lectures are best delivered face-to-face, since there are other ways I can establish my presence in the course. In the following, I examine my treatment of each of these three forms of course content as I redesigned the course for blended delivery.

Content: Texts

In general, I have found no good textbooks for SWC. This is not surprising, given its typical status in the anthropology program, which renders it marginal to the introductory course for the major. There are good (and very expensive) texts for an introductory cultural anthropology course but none for a survey of the sort I describe here. There are two alternatives to text-books most faculty adopt: one is to select several book-length ethnographies, the other is to use one of the half dozen or so readers in cultural anthropology now available on the market. I've tried selecting several ethnographies, but the increasing price of books has made it less and less feasible to assign more than two ethnographies (Remember: This is a *world* survey of cultures.) without facing a student revolt. An equally significant problem with the study of monographs is that students are often not up to the standard of reading that permits them to appreciate an argument sustained over several hundred pages. One of the course design choices I reluctantly made was not to introduce my students to the art and skill involved in reading full-length ethnographies. I ultimately decided that mastering the ethnographic genre was a task for anthropology majors, not general education enrollees.

This left readers in anthropology as my major potential source of text content. As I sat down with these readers, I became less and less satisfied with any one of them as a single text for the course. Each reader had several good articles (in the sense that I found the articles relevant, accessible, and brief); each reader also had quite a few articles that I disliked or even disagree with. I wound up deciding to choose articles from a broad range of sources including popular and academic journals, then have them converted to a digital format (Adobe PDF) and placed on electronic reserve. The articles would then be available via Web links on our local course management system, which is password protected to mitigate concerns of copyright infringement and appropriate fair use.

The pedagogical advantages of this approach are many, but of course from the students' perspective cost is almost always a significant factor, and to make the articles available for the cost of printing them or simply viewing them online allowed students easy access to their reading. From my own perspective, I could select articles that were appropriate to the areas I wished to cover and to the learning activities I intended for students to pursue. I note that in this context the advent of Google Scholar has been invaluable, since many full-text articles are immediately available online.

Content: Videos

The use of videos in cultural anthropology is a sine qua non of acquiring a diverse cultural experience, so my courses are invariably saturated with videos of various sorts, for example, ads, full-length scholarly treatments of particular exotic cultures, independent films. I have already mentioned that videos provide a learning environment many students are most comfortable with, but I want to go on to say that videos can provide the core of learning activities and high levels of student engagement as well. I briefly describe three ways I use videos to provoke student learning.

Televised commercials are especially evocative I've found. Since students are typically quite familiar with them, these ads allow the use of one or more defamiliarization exercises that immediately turn students into critical observers of their own culture. For instance, I've used Super Bowl ads (an area in which I have published several articles) to illustrate such culturally based matters as gender and racial bias, the defining of masculinities, and the significance of humor in exposing underlying cultural contradictions (e.g., Aycock & Duncan, 2009). Ads are especially convenient for this purpose because most are only 30 seconds long, which allows me to draw a maximum of cultural interpretation for the cost of very little time. They are also easy to present either online or face-to-face, all the more so now because of websites such as iFilm.com that archive all Super Bowl commercials.

Another way I've been able to make video central to my blended course design is to "rehearse" students before a video is seen in class by requiring them to view pertinent websites online before they come to class, then complete a simple learning activity that establishes their comprehension before they ever see the video. For instance, I often include a module on consumerism and globalization in SWC, because I think it is a subject that affects their lives significantly, yet it's often misrepresented in the media. Using Walmart as an example, I ask the students to view selected websites and take a quiz on some of their more controversial aspects, such as gender discrimination and other highly questionable labor practices, undermining of small local businesses, and cultural censorship. Alternatively, students may post a comment on a discussion forum about their own Walmart experiences in light of their reading. The students then view a piece on Walmart such as *Is Wal-Mart Good for America?* (Young, 2004). While they do so, they must take notes on eight to twelve controversies I have identified in the video for subsequent classroom debriefing. It's important, I think, not to approach video the way our teachers did in grade school, where the video was an opportunity for the teacher to catch up on grading and the students to catch up on sleep. I always give my students an assignment to complete that requires them to pay attention to the video and to take notes they will later submit for grading. In the video just mentioned, I require students to make a case for and against aspects of Walmart, then compare its cultural, political, and economic influence with that of other consumer giants such as McDonald's or Disney theme parks. One of our debriefings was so successful it wound up on Wikipedia under the entry "Walmarting" (Aycock & Aycock, 2008).

Content: Lectures

A third kind of learning activity is using videos to develop a kind of critical visual literacy that students usually lack. For instance, I may ask them to compare the use of light and shadow in two videos or the use of narration or the film editor's control over the pace of the film as a way to persuade students to perceive a video as something that is constructed through and through, in the same way our daily visual experience is continuously shaped and produced by our culture. To prepare such a learning activity, I may use excerpts from one or both of the films that are available online, together with critical reviews of the film from the Movie Review Query Engine (mrqe.com), the filmography from the Internet Movie Database (imdb.com), or other online materials such as interviews with the actors or filmmakers. I note once more that the availability of many films wholly or partly online via YouTube has made this task of rehearsal—initial contact with pertinent course material before entering the classroom—increasingly manageable, since it is no longer necessary for me to digitize the video clips myself.

I think lectures are highly overrated. They can be an efficient way to transfer information from the instructor to the student, but the traditional lecture offers little evidence that the student has heard what the lecturer intended or that the student has understood the lecture in any meaningful way. I've heard a number of faculty (including myself from time to time) describe themselves as good lecturers, but at this stage in my career I'm inclined to view such personal acclamations as vanity at best and perhaps less charitably a prima facie case for poor pedagogical understanding.

Having unburdened myself of these opinions, I should explain my reasoning. Lecturing works well when complex material can benefit from questioning and clarification in a face-to-face setting. Note, however, that if students have already encountered the material online, this elucidation may be even more effective, since students will often have had an opportunity to determine where their understanding needs a response from the instructor. Furthermore, the ability to review a lecture repeatedly online means that students may be able to figure out on their own the less-important areas that need clarifying, saving time in the classroom to focus on more important issues.

Another way to think about lectures is to ask whether multiple channels of communication—body language, vocal cues—are actually required to convey the information effectively. If the answer is no, as is often the case, then an underlying principle of economy suggests that the lecture material can be presented more conveniently in a different setting. The following factors led me to reconsider drastically how I would lecture in SWC.

First of all, I realized that indeed there was no good reason for students to listen to me recite my lecture notes, so I simply wrote them out word for word as if I were preparing a script. This was a significant effort, since I rarely use lecture notes at all, but I found that as I did this I clarified my own thinking about what I intended to say. I could also present the material in a more nuanced fashion, since it's quite possible for students to understand, say, complex clauses they are reading contrasted with an oral presentation where brevity is preferable. Once I had written the lectures, nothing prevented me from delivering them in the face-to-face classroom should I decide I needed to do so. The word-processed lectures also satisfied concerns about accessibility that are rarely addressed by those who prefer to offer live lectures.

Second, though, I wanted to give my students more of the context of a lecture than I would typically have the time to do in a face-to-face setting. It's valuable to be able to talk about where anthropological ideas come from, why I take a particular position or employ a specific methodology, and what key questions remain to be dealt with. For instance, why are anthropologists obsessed with kinship and marriage? What might be a good approach to understanding a story of marital strife—I often use the story of Judah and Tamar here—and how does this approach illuminate our present-day experience of marriage and family?

All this information often gets buried in or excluded from a live lecture. So I decided to include a brief (5–10 minutes) online introduction to each of the lectures: I recorded my remarks using voice-over PowerPoint, then rendered the resultant very large file as a compressed Flash file that would be smaller and more accessible via streaming. So I really had decided to have it both ways: a static Microsoft Word document provided the basic content in a form the students could download and study, while the more dynamic Flash introduction gave my students a sense that I was speaking directly to them, perhaps in a more intimate way than in the classroom. I note, however, that I typically omit clip art or a photo of myself or other graphics in the voice-over PowerPoint so my voice is the main point of contact between myself and the students. Orality of this sort has been identified theoretically and in empirical studies as an effective way of reducing the distancing effect of text-based materials (Ice, Curtis, Phillips, & Wells, 2007; Ong, 1982).

Moving the lectures out of the face-to-face portion of the course frees up a substantial amount of time for me to engage the students in ways that had not been possible before. For instance, I can now go into specific case studies or theoretical detail that would have been impossible if the students were encountering this material for the first time face-to-face. I have much greater expectations that students' answers to my questions will be more sophisticated—or for that matter, that they actually have an answer at all. I can devote time in class to small-group work when I wish. Most important for SWC, as I have already mentioned, I can show more videos to broaden the students' cultural experience.

In the following sections on assessment and engagement I discuss what I actually do in the face-to-face classroom. Before I leave my discussion of content, though, I want to observe that rethinking my content delivery has altered for the better the voice associated with the course. In a traditional lecture, the only voice to be heard is that of the instructor (and through the instructor, the text). Redesigning how I deliver content opens up a space for student voices to be heard as well (Aycock, 2003). I think the dialogic effect of blended learning, in which students participate in the course as active learners, is especially appropriate to a democratic society where civic participation is available as a responsibility and a privilege of the academy (Holquist, 2002, Chapter 6).

It's not enough, of course, to make it possible for student voices to be heard. My task as instructor is to help students learn how to develop their own voices. I now turn to my use of assessment in SWC.

ASSESSMENT

In a traditional course with relatively large enrollments, assessment of student work often amounts to no more than the three exams and a term paper arrangement we're all familiar with from our own undergraduate days. There's nothing wrong with exams or discursive writing; it's just that we know now that the best learning results can be obtained by using a much expanded and accelerated assessment repertoire (Walvoord & Anderson, 1998). Based on the literature and my own experiences, I follow some helpful general principles when I design my assessment plan for a blended course.

First of all, high-stakes testing is unreliable and a poor predictor or correlate of student understanding. High-stakes testing undermines students' efforts to improve their understanding, because it's typically a one-time event with little or no further opportunity to review and demonstrate learning of the content. It also creates an uneven rhythm in the course, in which students work very hard immediately before an exam but otherwise find themselves free to ignore whatever they might be learning if they were paying continuous attention to the course. By contrast, frequent low-stakes assessments let students know where they need to concentrate their efforts and encourage them (in fact, require them) to remain involved with the course materials on a routine day-to-day basis. In SWC students can expect to be assessed several times per week: it is usual for me to have 40–50 assessment items per student during a semester. A persistent comment on my course evaluations is students' admission (or plaint?) that mine was the only course in which they were fully caught up with their reading. This does mean that as a consequence I have to take my own workload quite seriously, as noted in more detail later.

A second principle of blended assessment is rapid turnaround. In SWC, I normally turn around assignments within 24–48 hours. Again I infer a kind of civic engagement between students and instructor: Each takes responsibility for a share of the course, which builds trust and a sense of common fate as an integral part of the learning community. By contrast, the traditional three exams and a term paper format was extremely slow-paced. As students we could expect a week or two to elapse between a major exam and a grade; in the meantime, the course had moved on and whatever had been learned or not been learned was no longer particularly relevant. Typically, end-of-term papers were graded after the semester had ended, so not only would it be too late to improve them for a further assessment, the students might well never even see them again until the following semester had begun, if then. The blended learning environment, on the other hand, is fast paced and—as I observed previously—dialogic. The instructor and student engage in a continuous series of transactions in which the student submits work to be assessed and the instructor replies rapidly with comments and suggestions for improvement. Use of assessment techniques that encourage a broad base of class participation results in the creation of a learning environment that is enriched by students' comments to one another, as well as by my own feedback.

A third principle of blended assessment is in some ways the most essential. As you may well imagine, the potential exists for the grading workload to overwhelm the instructor, particularly in large classes of 60–80 students. This means above all that I have to make my expectations for performance in any learning activity absolutely clear to my students and to myself. Not only does this focus my students' attention on what is important, it also gives me a systematic basis for assessment. I do two things to ensure that my expectations are explicit and easy to translate into a score or grade: I use rubrics for everything, and I grade these low-stakes assignments with as few decision points (e.g., 0, 1, 2 points) as possible. The first of these forces me to break away from my hidden expectations of how students will satisfy the requirements of their assignment. The second allows me to blur the scoring boundaries a bit, since it is my firm belief that trying to award closely measured point values (86.75/100, for instance) is far too precise when I am grading what amounts to a personal narrative. I should add that I always build in means to mitigate isolated occasions of poor performance, catastrophic personal or family events, and the like. Students can drop several of their lowest assignments, and ample opportunities are provided for small amounts of extra credit. This keeps the students in the game as it were, and avoids adversarial debates over trivial amounts of course credit.

So what do I actually assess in SWC? Everything, basically. If students are assigned to read or view course materials online, I give them an online quiz to ensure they've done it. If a module invites students to reflect upon their own experience—with work, with family celebrations, with the media— then the students record this experience in a discussion forum. In the face-to-face portion of the course, students must enter with a completed assignment and leave with another to complete for the next session.

I think what's at stake here is a question I am frequently asked: How do you know students are learning in a blended course? One answer is to offer data on retention and grades. Another response, although more combative, is to ask in return: How do you know students are learning in a purely face-to-face course? We often assume students learn best in a traditional environment, but if you compare the two, there is more evidence for student learning in a blended course than there is in a face-to-face course. How can three exams and a term paper possibly tell you as much about a student's learning as 40–50 assessment items? Good assessment requires students to produce *artifacts* of their learning—remember, I'm an anthropologist—and these artifacts are more extensive in a blended course than they could ever be in a purely face-to-face class.

Scalability, as I've mentioned, comes fully into play. The use of clickers in lieu of a hard-copy entrance assignment, I will argue, essentially allows students to record their own grades at the same time they participate in the course dialogue. The use of online quizzing graded by our course management system checks on students' learning of key concepts and basic recall of ethnographic examples. Breaking up a longer assignment (e.g., an ethnographic outing at the mall) into several pieces means that students gain their feedback throughout the semester, and the instructor isn't struggling to grade 80 hastily scribbled papers long after the semester has been completed.

My point is that my assessment plan in SWC is characteristic of a blended course: frequent, low stakes, and rapid turnaround. This approach to assessment is fully consistent with values underlying the delivery of content that seek to foreground the role of continuous engagement as a means to ensure students are active participants in their own learning. The online and face-to-face components of SWC strengthen the connection between assessment and engagement and promote the development of a learning community in both aspects of the course.

ENGAGEMENT ONLINE: DISCUSSION FORUMS

For courses in the social sciences and humanities whose framework is typically discursive, I regard asynchronous discussion forums as the principle tool of learning and assessment. One advantage of discussion forums is that students can reflect at leisure and bring new materials to the table, either from cultural experience or from the vast quantity of information available on the Web. If you do it right, pedagogically speaking, posting comments on discussion forums guarantees that virtually all students will participate and apply what they have learned to their own experience or to examples chosen by them. Given this increased level of engagement, it is also more likely they will produce a well-formed scholarly argument that includes theory and empirical examples.

What discussion assignments work best online? I always try to assign questions that are in some sense edgy, that have more than one answer. Asking questions that merely invite students to recite their readings is pointless; instead, think about the nature of a face-to-face conversation in class or a scholarly argument. The key to students' interest is that the exchanges are open-ended, replete with shades of meaning that can be explored. Specific examples can be examined from every angle over and over again and important issues thoroughly debated. Because it sustains itself in the tangible form of the forum, online discourse, I would argue, is actually superior to its live counterpart.

Here are some examples. If the students are reading a particular article or chapter, I'll give them a quote from that reading and ask them why the author found it necessary to include that statement as part of the argument. Or I'll give them a quote from one author, and ask whether another author whose work they are reading would agree or disagree with that quote and why. A third variant asks the students why they should believe this quote, that is, what evidence does the author provide, what are its limitations, what else would we have to know to decide whether the author's position could be upheld? I often divide the class into smaller groups, which permits me to ask different questions of each group or to take a general problem (such as truth telling in fieldwork) and see how several groups might independently approach the solution to that problem.

Asking students to apply their own experience to a theoretical model can be rewarding so long as the model is not too complex, and so long as your rubric stresses the importance of fluent personal narrative as a source of ethnographic insight. I find students are quite willing to disclose their own experience (sometimes too much), but they must sometimes be coaxed to elaborate on what seems to them to be obvious and scarcely worth mentioning. In this latter case, a word limit can offer an opportunity to ask for more detail (and I note that using the words *imaginative, vivid, intriguing,* or similar adjectives less commonly encountered in university rubrics, can inspire students to embellish their stories accordingly). I think this qualitative approach can be applicable in many fields other than social and cultural anthropology. For instance, during my career I have taught courses in sociology, religious studies, and women's studies in which I applied a qualitative approach to good effect. As Rorty famously remarked of the humanities and social sciences, the point is "to keep the conversation going" (Rorty, 1979, p. 377).

Familiarizing students with the process of posting comments on a discussion forum is vital to their later success. I always begin my course with a simple online exercise, such as a personal introduction or a brief ethnographic observation, that accustoms students to posting and makes sure they have the technical resources to succeed. For instance, I'll give my students Horace Miner's classic "Body Ritual Among the Nacirema" (1956) and ask them to pretend they are Martian anthropologists sent to observe and describe a body ritual of the Nacirema (Americans). I ask them to introduce themselves by telling the class what they do for fun, whether they've ever lived in a different culture (whatever *difference* means to them at this stage), and selecting their own favorite YouTube video for everyone to see.

I grade these assignments very quickly, with an eye to making sure the students have followed the simple rules I have laid out (e.g., 350 words, 1 point for answering each question about themselves, extra credit for including a picture). They quickly get the idea this is not superfluous to the course; it is a part of the course they will participate in on a routine basis, so they need to include it in their plans. At the same time, incidentally, I may ask the students to take their first online quiz so they realize my expectations for their reading: The quiz questions are only true/false and multiple choice, but they are timed in such a way (30–45 seconds per question) that the answers have to be known in advance for the students to complete the quiz on time.

I have used group work more frequently as I have become more comfortable with the blended mode of teaching and learning. I typically divide the class into groups of 8–10 students for their online discussions to create a more intimate, manageable environment and to allow multiple discussions of the same topic to play themselves out independently without exhausting the lines of conversation. I also am very specific about the requirement to respond to one another (and the tenor of that response), as well as about the timing of posting and responding. It's critical to make student postings on the forum a part of their regular routine rather than something they hurry to get out of the way as quickly as possible in the most perfunctory way. I have found the face-to-face class becomes subsequently richer and more rewarding if each of the online small groups has its own contribution to make, independent of the whole. Even when I used to use small-group work during a traditional face-to-face class, the small groups never became as cohesive as they do if they have worked together online prior to their reporting in the larger face-to-face setting.

To reduce the workload associated with numerous postings, I employ two strategies. First I require students to discuss a topic in their own small group but then post a composite or summary response in a forum accessible to the entire class. That allows me to skim the intragroup postings to learn how students are pursuing their task and to ensure each is making a serious contribution, while paying more careful attention to the overall conclusions that arise from these initial detailed conversations. My corresponding assessment technique is to provide only a point or so for the private group work, merely to confirm that everyone participated, but to allocate a greater number of points to the group for the summary posting. (Remember, of course, these discussions are a prelude to the ensuing face-to-face class meeting where group participation is further rewarded.) A second strategy is to devise a rubric that actually satisfies my own idea of what I would like to read online. Of course I include the formalities—theory, empirical examples—but I also include the intangibles: Does your posting sound as if you were actually interested in the topic or just trying to get by? Is it interesting to read? Am I entertained or surprised? In other words, I can use the rubric to guide my expectations and theirs in considerable detail, and the rule of thumb is, the more thoroughly you discuss your expectations about an assignment, the richer the students' responses will be.

Finally, it's also important to consider what the instructor's voice will be in a discussion forum and in giving feedback to students. Will the instructor respond to everyone or only to some? Does an instructor's response to a student mean he or she has done especially well or especially poorly? Is the instructor an agent provocateur, or are instructor postings to be taken at face value? It really doesn't matter what the instructor decides in this regard, but it is important that students know what to expect. There seem to be two kinds of instructors: hands off and hands on. I belong to the latter category, in part out of sheer compulsiveness, but more because I think my participation in the routine give-and-take of discussion is a guarantor of the students' taking it seriously. At the same time, I've heard persuasive arguments that in at least some forums, faculty prefer to be hands off to require students to assume an active learning role even in the instructor's temporary absence. Either way, however, the point is to make the discussion forums valuable to students' learning and to ensure that students take them seriously. This means that discussions must be a significant part of the assessment plan for the course, which also leads me to my final comment on discussion forums.

Many faculty ask how to grade discussion forums and worry about the extra workload this sort of feedback imposes. This is a reasonable concern; fortunately, there is an excellent repertoire of time-saving practices to draw from. I have already spoken of rubrics and the advantages of low-stakes postings with few decision points (essentially grading on a pass-fail basis). For more substantive feedback, I have adopted a policy of reading a dozen or so postings, then composing half a dozen paragraphs, each of which addresses a different characteristic flaw in a typical posting. I can then use these paragraphs as a core of my remarks as I work my way through the grade book. I just copy and paste the appropriate paragraph into the feedback area that the student will see and add a remark or two that personalizes it and takes account of individual contributions. It's very simple and effective to offer feedback this way and helps students to learn the art of writing (very) short essays.

I now move to the face-to-face portion of the course.

ENGAGEMENT FACE-TO-FACE: CLASSROOM ASSESSMENT TECHNIQUES (CATs) AND CLICKERS

I use two principal tools in the face-to-face component of the course to ensure a high level of engagement and feedback—CATs and clickers.

CATs

CATs, pioneered and made popular by Angelo and Cross (1993), briefly put, are very short—typically one-page—assignments in which students respond to a question that reveals the extent of their learning or the tenor of their response to a particular module of course content. By contrast with *summative* tools, such as final exams or final course evaluations, CATs are always *formative* or *progressive* assessments that occur during the learning process and therefore evoke a quality of immediacy that promotes rapid feedback (the hallmark of blended learning) and multiple voices in the classroom. I normally use two subtypes of CATs, entrance and exit tickets.

Entrance tickets are one-and-a-half- to two-page word-processed documents each student submits upon entering the classroom. Because the submissions are word processed, they cannot be hastily written as the student walks into the room; the student must write and print the document prior to class, requiring at least a modicum of preparation and reflection. Because they are required to be submitted in person—I don't accept them by e-mail or in my mailbox, even prior to the class—the student has to attend the face-to-face class to hand it to me. Thus the entrance assignment acts as a proxy for class attendance (as we'll see, the exit assignment performs the same task at the end of class). I think this is preferable to the usual requirement of attendance and participation, which inevitably becomes a fudge factor and all too readily lends itself to unconscious discrimination.

Although entrance tickets can be written on any topic, I usually tie them to the reading for that day. I'm not looking for a straightforward summary of the reading. Instead, I ask the students to prepare an argument that relates to the reading and often to their own experience as well. For instance, if I have assigned a couple of articles on household dynamics in a matrilineal or a polyandrous society, I may ask them to make a case for their being more comfortable in one of these societies than the other and to give their reasons, citing the article and their own experience of marriage. I might ask them to decide whether the author of an article has a sufficient basis for a claim that bribery is an acceptable cultural norm in Bolivia, or whether another author who critiques American foreign aid in Lesotho would agree that a similar cultural process has contributed to the de-skilling of workers in the midwestern United States. Sometimes, for variety's sake, I'll ask several questions and ask them to choose one to answer. Initially, students have difficulty developing a series of claims and sustaining them with evidence, but after they have written a few and received good feedback from me, their task goes more quickly and they become fluent in the genre of academic debate. I do provide students up front with a clear rationale for this departure from the usual end-of-semester term paper, and I have found they eventually come to value the clarity and focus of brief argumentation.

Entrance tickets produce a classroom conversation that is invariably richer and more sophisticated. If the students' "first exposure" (Walvoord & Anderson, 1998, pp. 53–57) to the course material is when they sit down and take out their notebooks, a lot of the class time is wasted bringing everyone up to speed on the basics of the reading assignment for that day. Alternatively, if I proceed as if everyone did their reading, only a few members of the class are in fact equipped to contribute to class discussion. The entrance assignment guarantees that at least the students have done *some* reading pertinent to the day's content, and even they have had to reflect on it to be able to answer the question(s) I have posed for them. A more complex level of critical reasoning can now come into play, starting from the work that has already been completed.

Entrance tickets also reduce that killer of classroom discussion, freezing up, with the accompanying frantic deer-in-the-headlights look you get when you call on someone who hasn't the least idea of what is going on. Students who have handed in their entrance ticket have at least something to say about the topic at hand. In more difficult class discussions, I allow the students to hang on to their entrance assignment when they walk in and hand them in partway through the class.

Finally, entrance assignments are easy to grade. I maintain the overall value of the assignment at a relatively low level, usually 3 points per submission, which gives me a sufficient range to grade the papers seriously but doesn't commit me to a full-scale assessment process. Of course, I use a (much simplified) rubric for grading to maintain consistency and cut down on the amount of writing I must do in return. Simply stapling the rubric to the original paper with a couple of freehand comments usually suffices to give students some guidance for future writing of the same sort.

Despite these assessment shortcuts, and as the enrollment for SWC rose from 40 to 60 to 80 students, I eventually found that turning around the entrance assignments for the following class became somewhat onerous. For this reason I switched from using entrance assignments to using clickers to accomplish similar pedagogical goals.

Exit assignments have pedagogical purposes somewhat similar to entrance tickets, but there are important differences as well. By exit assignment I mean a handwritten one-paragraph response to a question posed during the face-to-face class itself (Aycock, 2006). The students submit the exit assignment as they leave the room at the end of class.

One purpose of an exit assignment is, again, to ensure attendance. Thus the entrance and exit assignments taken together define attendance and participation in a relatively unequivocal manner that is much more evenhanded than the traditional fudge factor approach. Another purpose, clearly enough, is to encourage engagement, since it's hard for a student to check out mentally and still compose a coherent paragraph about the day's discussion.

Less obvious is the importance of the immediacy of the exit assignment. I am trying to gauge the cognitive and emotional aspects of the learning that has taken place during the past 75 minutes. Are they intrigued by what they have learned? Perhaps even better, are they moved or disturbed by it? I have found in SWC that students typically answer from the gut when they have little time to process or gain distance from an issue. This stands in contrast to the entrance assignment, where creating distance is part of the point of the exercise.

In addition, I note two further uses of exit assignments. I can request an exit assignment halfway through the class rather than at its conclusion, allowing students time to rehearse a discussion on the topic. For instance, in a module on wage labor in the modern economy I usually ask students to write down a few sentences about the crappiest job they've ever had. Now one thing I know about my students is that they have all had bad jobs, in fact most of them still have those jobs, trying to pay their way through college. Another thing I know is my students have a keen sense of injustice, so the *crappiest* descriptor of the assignment is meant to draw on their emotional reaction to their perception of the unfairness of it all, as well as the diversity of jobs (most of which do indeed sound pretty awful). Now that I've given the class 10 minutes or so to write this exit assignment, I can call on individual students with considerable confidence, since no matter how shy they are, they still have an answer written down in front of them that they can read off to the class. An important conclusion to this class activity is my summary of the exit assignment once the class is over. I choose the students' own descriptive words to produce an overview—from a native perspective—of the microethnography of crappy jobs. From this I draw the obvious conclusions about the Marxist critique of wage labor and the nuances of alienation expressed in the students' writing. I post this summary on the course website. The next class begins with this summary for review and to emphasize the broader theoretical context involved in our everyday cultural experiences, and continues from there to develop further experiences or to make a transition to a related topic, such as the evolution of centralized and stratified political organizations.

Here again I follow some general principles in such assignments. First, their immediacy and relative informality contributes to the comfortable environment I wish to establish in the face-to-face classroom. I'm avoiding the formal, somewhat stifling, traditional lecture arrangement where the students sit trapped in their seats while I pontificate. Second, I insist that the students participate in their own learning, rather than sleeping, spacing out, texting, or talking with their friends. Again, my voice is not the only one heard in the classroom. Third, the grading process involves rapid turnaround and minimum risk to the students. I usually grade exit assignments on a 0, 1, 2 basis: If the student did well, then 2 points is in order; if OK, then it's 1 point; if the student blew it off, he or she gets 0 points. So there's just enough course credit involved to get the students to take it seriously but not enough for them to fight about. I can grade the 80 exit assignments for SWC in about an hour.

Exit assignments can also be used to get feedback on whether the students understand the material being addressed or more generally on how the course is going so far. For example, I may ask, "What is the muddiest point?" meaning what single item in today's material did they find the most difficult to understand. I can then address that point in detail. Another exit assignment is, "What is one thing you like about this course so far?" and "What is one thing you'd like to fix?" which asks for a balanced assessment of the course, usually about 6 weeks into the semester. Once more, I always post a summary of the responses, and I always look for a few things that I can indeed fix so the students know they have a say in how the class is being taught. I think it's important to create a sense of reciprocity between myself and the students: They give me their ideas in their exit assignments, and I reciprocate by summarizing and answering their needs.

I now turn to my other face-to-face engagement tool, clickers.

Clickers

Clickers are a system that captures student responses synchronously during a live face-to-face class; then displays the results graphically. Clickers have several advantages technically and socially. First of all, students are entering their own data electronically, so the instructor doesn't have to. Second, since each student response is recorded and identifiable, instructors can have, in effect, student attendance, attention, and participation very straightforwardly. Third, students can make their responses to the instructor's prompts or questions without revealing their identity publicly and risking embarrassment, and at the same time they are able to see how everyone else has responded. This property of clickers removes one of the major obstacles to student engagement and class participation.

Clickers are quite flexible in terms of the pedagogy involved. I can ask questions that require simple recall of key concepts or examples from readings, which is a low-level cognitive task that nevertheless makes sure the students have done their reading, for example: What percentage of societies permit polygyny? What ratio best represents the respective contributions to the family meal of women and men in a hunter-gatherer or foraging society?

I can also ask students to predict the outcome of an ethnographic study or to choose among contending explanations for a cultural phenomenon, which is a slightly higher-level question. For instance, I could ask, "Do American marriages tend toward endogamy? Let's check out your initial prediction via clickers." Then I can poll the class in detail to discover whether their own parents married endogamously or whether they themselves have. Or I could take an example from the reading: "If Scheper-Hughes (1992) believes emotions are culturally prescribed, while Wikan (1990) believes emotions are innate, which argument do you find the most persuasive in terms of the data they present?" The answers to these questions can be amplified and debated following the initial recording of responses.

I use the think-pair-share technique for more extended clicker questions. I'll ask students to take a position, making some notes for themselves in the process, then discuss their reasoning with the person next to them. I invite a public class discussion of the arguments for or against, then finally repoll the students to see whether their ideas have changed. For instance, I used this technique when I wanted the class to consider whether Christian Communion could be considered—as most anthropologists would argue—a form of ritual cannibalism. Students had to examine their own religious experience and attempt to reconcile it with the use of an alien (and for many, insulting) anthropological concept. This proved an excellent opportunity to illustrate the role of theory in anthropology and the problem of using concepts that didn't represent native constructions. This use of clickers is, as you can tell, potentially a much higher order of cognition as well as deeply engaging for the class.

Finally, I use clickers for feedback during a class or toward its conclusion, to find out which part of that day's work was the muddiest (unclear), or which part the students found emotionally the most challenging, or which part the students would like to pursue in more depth. I can then use this feedback to begin a further explanation of a difficult topic, to extend the issues to a later face-to-face class meeting, or to set the stage for an online assignment.

Naturally, clicker systems differ somewhat from one another, though overall their functionality is fairly standard. I do want to offer a technical and a pedagogical observation. Technically, I've found it's important to take steps to support students' use of clickers and their confidence that their answers are being properly recorded. Otherwise, students may feel their responses are being cast into a deep dark hole, since they have no easy way to tell whether I've received them. Pedagogically, I've learned that the use of clickers should always be low stakes, and if a concern arises, it's preferable to err on the side of generosity if students feel they have been deprived of credit they deserve. The technical and pedagogical implications of clickers have to be dealt with carefully if students are to embrace their use with the enthusiasm that translates to engagement. And incidentally, I never use clickers to take attendance, as students' attendance is implicit in their responses. Studies clearly show that students resent the use of clickers merely to satisfy a sort of bureaucratic formalism (Kaleta & Joosten, 2007).

One thing about clickers that is rather subtle, yet goes to the foundation of a course redesigned for blended learning, is that they have the capacity to break up the steady flow of a lecture and alter the rhythm of a face-to-face class. Clickers intrinsically imply there are multiple voices in the classroom. As I've already observed, a key element in redesigning my SWC course for blended teaching and learning was to give up the notion that only I had a voice worth listening to in the course.

ASSESSMENT AND ENGAGEMENT: A SUMMARY PERSPECTIVE

I summarize my narrative up to this point by saying that I usually have an overall assessment plan that comprises several types of learning activities that foster engagement:

- online quizzes and exams, multiple choice and true/false
- online discussion forum postings based on personal ethnography
- entrance and exit assignments
- clicker questions and responses

Students must remain involved with the course throughout, since each class and each week of the course contains multiple assessments. At the same time no single assessment item is high-stakes (the two or three exams are around 15 points each, while all the other items are 2–5 points apiece out of an overall total of 100 points), so if a student has a crisis of some sort, or does poorly in one part of the course, there is still plenty of time to make up the work on other occasions. I note in passing that I allow students to drop one or more of their lowest grades in each type of assignment (our course management system can do this automatically and recalculate the result) so I don't have to deal with excuses, disputes, or makeups.

Once all is said and done, I am fairly confident that my students learn more from this approach to assessment and that they are deeply engaged with the course materials and with one another. This confidence is in some sense purely circumstantial: During 40 years of teaching, I lectured for the first 5 years, introduced more and more elements of active learning during the next 15 or so, then finally moved entirely to blended and fully online learning in the mid-1990s. In retrospect, I don't see how I could have been satisfied with the limited range of assessments that preceded my conversion to blended and online learning—and I would never go back. More to the point, my intuitive response is strongly reflected in studies of blended learning I am familiar with (Aycock, Garnham, & Kaleta, 2002; Kaleta, Skibba, & Joosten, 2008).

INTEGRATING FACE-TO-FACE AND ONLINE: DESIGNING A MODULE

As I write about each element of the course, I think it's easy to lose sight of the larger picture, so here I describe how I design a course module, and what I believe to be the benefits of a blended mode of online and face-to-face work.

A course module includes an amalgam of content, learning activities, and an assessment protocol. At least some of the components appear online and at least some function face-to-face.

My goal in designing a module is to avoid the very common error of teaching a blended course that has two separate and parallel components, one online and one face-to-face, and the two parts of the course operate independently and in isolation from one another. Inevitably in such a situation, the online part of the course is perceived (often by the instructor as well as by the students) as icing on the cake or busy work rather than as an integral mode of teaching and learning, so the online part of the course is marginalized while the face-to-face part is implicitly considered—in large part because it is traditional—to be where the real or authentic instruction and learning occur. The model of a blended course requires integration between face-to-face and online learning activities, so that each can inform, elaborate, and extend the other. I now outline a repertoire for a typical module, then describe how I use it.

The example I use here is my Islam module. I developed this module specifically for SWC because I knew my students were curious about Islam and also (rightly) suspicious of the media characterization of Muslims. Many of the students in my class are from a conservative Christian background, which further complicates their understanding of and reaction to Muslims. In some sense I think it's my job in SWC to present situations where students find themselves culturally uncomfortable or disoriented. The way I guide them to work through their malaise is characteristic of anthropology in general but is also facilitated by a blended approach.

Here's a list of all my activities for the module on Islam. Most of these can either function face-to-face or online:

- Hasan's (2002) nicely crafted memoir of growing up as an American Muslim
- online websites focused on Islam (e.g., Islamicity or Islam 101)
- brief YouTube videos on Islam (e.g., Chechnyan Sufis, http://www.youtube.com/watch?feature = player_detailpage&v = Q3xP4nfDkzc; or the Muslim hip-hop of Clotaire K, http://www.youtube.com/watch?feature = player_detailpage&v = xAZ_niqSrHA)
- a quiz, multiple choice and true/false, on the details of Islamic belief (e.g., Do Muslims believe Christ was crucified? Are most Muslims Arabic? What does the word *Qu'ran* actually mean?)
- videos on various aspects of Islam, such as *Paradise Lies at the Feet of the Mother* (Percival, 1993), which deals with Islamic women in Indonesia, Africa, and Egypt or *Saints and Spirits* (Fernea, 1979), which shows variants of Islam in Morocco
- inviting a local Muslim to speak to my class—in the past, I have invited a Palestinian woman, or a man who is an active member of the Nation of Islam

First, I assign some directed reading, either from the Hasan (2002) text or from standard websites on Islam. Second, I ask the students to demonstrate they've understood the reading by requiring them to take a quiz on the details of Islam. This quiz may occur online; alternatively, I may use clickers to give the quiz face-to-face so the students can discuss their answers. Third, I ask the students to view a video on Islam. Both of the videos mentioned in the list treat Islam realistically, as a culturally and historically situated set of practices and ideas rather than as a monolithic entity. The students are asked to display their mastery of the videos by taking notes to answer a series of questions. For instance, I may give them a list of a dozen questions, each representing a different scene in *Paradise Lies at the Feet of the Mother* and require them to decide which scene is more important for their own experience as Americans, or I ask them to decide how Hasan would characterize the scene if she saw the same video. Fourth, the students must prepare for the guest speaker by working online as a group to devise questions for the speaker and post them on a discussion forum. The questions are then posed to the speaker, and subsequently students post the answers to their questions on the discussion forum. If their questions remain unanswered, they may get credit for answering one another's questions, or I may suggest where to find the answer.

You can see this is not by any means a passive series of learning activities. Each stage of the module feeds into and elaborates the previous stage and prepares for the next. For example, the students move from an understanding of Islam at its most general level to an awareness of specific issues, such as the role of women, then finally to an evaluation of lived experience of practicing Muslims and of the students' own experience as Americans. At each stage, the students demonstrate their achievement of pedagogical goals I have identified by producing one or more artifacts that can be assessed. It's also significant, I think, that I use course material of many different types to accommodate quite different learning styles and to make sense of the particular environment best suited to a certain activity or item of content.

The length of course time for this module can vary, since I may set it up differently from one offering of SWC to another, for example, I may not have a guest speaker available for a particular course. The full sequence might require three weeks of face-to-face and online work, while a truncated sequence might last two weeks, or even a week and a half. I always take care to refer to each of the previous steps in a sequence and to bring into play the artifacts each student has produced and brought to the table. For instance, in class I like to review the most commonly missed quiz questions to find out why the students chose a wrong (or even a right) answer. I like to prompt a discussion of the students' reactions to their guest speaker as soon as possible afterward either online or face-to-face to allow them to fully describe their reactions in a way that makes it possible for the students to evaluate their own position as Americans more objectively or in a more nuanced fashion. The point is that the two components of the course are fully integrated, and the students' progress is measurable in terms of the artifacts of their learning.

CONCLUSION: LESSONS LEARNED AND NEW DIRECTIONS

At the time of this writing, I've offered SWC seven times, twice face-to-face (though with online activities on each occasion) and twice fully online. Three times I've taught it as a blended course. What have I learned? A more interesting question, perhaps, is which mode of instruction works better with SWC. Finally, what changes can I make to the course to improve it?

I think that among lessons learned I would include three in particular: Fostering the development of diverse voices in the course is important, an assessment plan that depends upon rapid, low-stakes feedback has value, and documenting learning at each juncture of the course is also valuable. Each of these, in my view, is strongly influenced—or even inherent—in blended learning as a mode of course delivery.

By fostering diverse voices I mean two things: breaking up the monolithic lecture/textbook voice of the instructor by the deliberate intrusion of briefer alternative media and opening up public spaces to make it possible for students to speak. My use of video clips and YouTube is an example of the former; using discussion forums and clickers is an example of the latter. The cumulative effect of hearing voices in this course is to engage students with their own learning as opposed to a far more passive disengagement common in traditional classes. Blended learning supplies many more sources for such diversity while (unlike online learning) retaining the traditional availability of live voices in the face-to-face classroom.

I think assessment is often underrated as a source of active learning, in large part because traditional high-stakes assessment is so glacial and unwieldy there is nothing active about it, and as I have remarked, neither students nor instructors are likely to associate grading with learning. It's more a method of punishment and a means to satisfy your department chair and the registrar at the end of the semester. But low-stakes assessment with rapid turnaround and ample feedback meets the goals of keeping the students on task, of letting students and the instructor know when things are going awry, and of sustaining the faster pace of the course. At the same time, instructors can use rubrics and CATs to maintain their own workload at a manageable level. The fast pace of assessment is partially accounted for by the use of online work, such as automated testing under the aegis of a course management system, and partially through approaches such as entrance and exit assignments that are most effectively addressed in a face-to-face setting.

The documentation of learning arises as students post comments on the discussion forums, record their clicker scores, submit their entrance and exit assignments, and even as they complete online quizzes or exams. I always have a complete record of a student's individual performance in SWC from the first week to the last, and at any point where students are falling short of meeting the course goals I can readily intervene to advise them where they stand and how they should proceed to improve their work. Students often remark in SWC course evaluations that they are surprised to find how well they and I know one another—in contrast to a traditional course—and how interesting it is to experience their peer learning communities online and face-to-face. In a nontrivial way, therefore, I think this documentation of learning (particularly discussion forums and clickers) has a somewhat unanticipated outcome: It makes visible a community of learners, while more traditional forms of assessment isolate students from one another. I note in passing that the value of the course is much more fully documented for the scrutiny of any interested third party such as the department curriculum committee or external accreditors. Although it can be argued that online courses are superior in their capacity to document learning, I say that the goal of fostering a community of learners is more readily achieved when online and face-to-face communities are shaped by documentation of learning in both. Each provides a distinct arena for the demonstration of learning that neither would supply by itself alone.

Which mode of instruction works best with SWC? A course management system to supplement the face-to-face classroom vastly improves some of the most important aspects of traditional learning—content delivery, assessment, and active learning. Further, the flexibility inherent in blended and online learning are instrumental in meeting the needs of the overwhelming percentage of students who are managing a job and a family while attending school.

As for differentiating between blended and online modes of teaching and learning, each has its advantages in principle. I'm distinguishing SWC from other courses in anthropology where lab work is an essential aspect of the course objectives making a fully online course impractical without undertaking the high production costs of rich interactive media.

Fully online learning maximizes the potential for convenience, since it separates the educational setting from a particular time or place. For instance, during the last online version of SWC, I had two students who were serving in the armed forces in Iraq and two other students who gave birth before the end of the semester. Online learning also produces nearly perfect documentation of the work of the course, which can prove valuable under a range of circumstances. Online learning, however, also entails a relatively high cost in course redesign that is heavily front loaded; that is, you've got to be ready to go with a 100% course redesign plan and have sufficient time to implement it. People almost always underestimate the time and effort required if they have never before taught fully or partially online courses. My rule of thumb is that you need three full months of course redesign time, and in fact SWC needed almost exactly three months to redesign from blended to fully online, even though I am fairly experienced in such tasks.

Although I appreciate the value of a fully online approach (and so do my students, according to my evaluations), I think for SWC, I would prefer to teach it as blended for a couple of reasons. First, a blended course entails a less thoroughgoing transformation than its fully online counterpart. You can construct a perfectly satisfactory blended course that is 30% to 40% online with relatively little effort, so long as you take care to integrate the online and face-to-face components. Second, a blended course is a work in progress in the best sense of that phrase. I perceive blended teaching and learning as highly experimental, permitting the instructor the freedom to try new ideas in a way that is far more difficult online. For instance, if I decide I want my students to try out a new pedagogical tool such as Second Life, I can lead them through the training more straightforwardly than if we were meeting only online. If the Second Life experiment is truncated for some reason, it is much easier to rearrange the course if it is being taught in blended mode. Third, some ideas and activities benefit from full body contact among students and instructor. I'd rather introduce my students to Foucault face-to-face so that I can engage students with his intricacies in a context that offers immediate feedback and allows me to target areas that require careful elaboration. Another example: Gaining students' instant response as I have prescribed for exit assignments makes more sense in a face-to-face environment where the keenness of their answers is not dulled by reflection.

Finally, what's next for SWC? I've mentioned that I'm already incorporating YouTube into my courses, but I would prefer for my students to develop their own audio and video for some mediated ethnographic projects. The ease and lowered cost of digital recording has made this option a great deal more accessible now. I've also mentioned Second Life, one example of the broader range of games and simulations that have recently become available for instructional purposes. My first take on games and simulations is that they lack the rich diversity characteristic of even the most mundane live situations, but that could change rapidly. In any case, I regard using games and simulations as one of those experiments the blended format so readily lends itself to. Last, I have not yet incorporated wikis or ePortfolios into my courses, in part because I have until now lacked the requisite software in the context of our campus course management system, and I believe strongly in one-stop shopping for the use of learning technologies. I have also not yet mastered sufficiently the pedagogy of small groups needed to use wikis in large enrollment courses. Yet I think these three areas for exploration speak so clearly to the fundamental values of blended learning—activity, interactivity, and learning community—that I should be remiss not to take advantage of them.

REFERENCES

Angelo, T., & Cross, P. (1993). *Classroom assessment techniques: A handbook for college teachers*. San Francisco, CA: Jossey-Bass.

Aycock, A. (2003). *Serendipity and SoTL: An ethnographic narrative*. In C. Schroeder & A. Ciccone (Eds.), *Learning more about learning* (pp. 25–38). Milwaukee: University of Wisconsin–Milwaukee Center for Instructional and Professional Development.

Aycock, A. (2006). "This way to the egress": Using exit assignments to improve communication in your course. In P. Rice & D. McCurdy (Eds.), *Strategies in teaching anthropology* (4th ed., pp. 34–39). Upper Saddle River, NJ: Prentice Hall.

Aycock, J., & Aycock, A. (2008). Why I love/hate wikipedia: Reflections upon (not quite) subjugated knowledges. *Journal of the Scholarship of Teaching and Learning, 8*(2), 92–101. Retrieved from https://www.iupui.edu/~josotl/archive/vol_8/no_2/v8n2aycock.pdf

Aycock, A., & Duncan, M. (2008). Super Bowl ad humor: At the intersections of race, class, and gender. In L. Wenner & S. Jackson (Eds.), *Sport, beer, and gender in promotional culture: Explorations of a holy trinity* (pp. 243–260). New York, NY: Peter Lang.

Aycock, A., Garnham, C., & Kaleta, R. (2002). Lessons learned from the hybrid course project. *Teaching With Technology Today, 8*(6). Retrieved from http://www.wisconsin.edu/ttt/articles/garnham2.htm

Bass, R. (1999). The scholarship of teaching: What's the problem? *Inventio, 1*(1). Retrieved from http://www.doiiit.gmu.edu/Archives/feb98/randybass.htm

Fernea, E. (Producer). (1979). *Saints and spirits* [DVD]. New York, NY: Icarus Films.

Hasan, A. (2002). *American Muslims* (2nd ed.). New York, NY: Continuum.

Holquist, M. (2002). *Dialogism: Bakhtin and his world* (2nd ed.). New York, NY: Routledge.

Ice, P., Curtis, R., Phillips, P., & Wells, J. (2007). Using asynchronous audio feedback to enhance teaching presence and students' sense of community. *Journal of Asynchronous Learning Networks, 11*(2), 1–23. Retrieved from http://sloancon sortium.org/sites/default/files/v11n2_ice_0.pdf

Kaleta, R., & Joosten, T. (2007). *Student response systems: A University of Wisconsin System study of clickers* [Research bulletin]. Retrieved from the Educause website: http://connect.educause.edu/Library/ECAR/StudentResponseSystemsAUn/40166

Kaleta, R., Skibba, K. A., & Joosten, T. (2008). Discovering, designing, and delivering hybrid courses. In A. Picciano & C. Dziuban (Eds.), *Blended learning: Research perspectives* (pp. 111–143). Needham, MA: Sloan Consortium.

Miner, H. (1956). Body ritual among the Nacirema. *American Anthropologist, 58,* 503–507.

Ong, W. (1982). *Orality and literacy: The technologizing of the word.* New York, NY: Methuen.

Percival, J. (1993). *Living Islam Vol. 4, Paradise lies at the feet of the mother.* New York, NY: Ambrose Video Publishing.

Rorty, R. (1979). *Philosophy and the mirror of nature.* Princeton, NJ: Princeton University Press.

Scheper-Hughes, N. (1992). *Death without weeping: The violence of everyday life in Brazil.* Los Angeles: University of California Press.

Walvoord, B., & Anderson, V. (1998). *Effective grading: A tool for learning and assessment.* San Francisco, CA: Jossey-Bass.

Wikan, U. (1990). *Managing turbulent hearts: A Balinese formulation for living.* Chicago, IL: University of Chicago Press.

Young, R. (Producer). (2004). *Is Wal-Mart good for America?* [Video webcast]. Retrieved from http://www.pbs.org/wgbh/pages/frontline/shows/walmart/

4

Combining Tradition With Technology
Redesigning a Literature Course

Tracey M. Gau

When I started teaching at the University of North Texas (UNT) 12 years ago, fresh out of graduate school, I began by teaching the mega-section of World Literature I. It was an auditorium-style room filled with 300 students, many of whom were non-English majors simply looking to fulfill a humanities requirement. Having graduated from a small, private university of 7,000 students, in which all the classes were held seminar style, I soon learned how to teach while some students slept, while some read the newspaper, while some did other homework, and while some just stared without anything in front of them at all. I realized then that my graduate school mentor's predictions were keenly accurate: First, although I would be a trained specialist, I would become a generalist expected to teach a broad range of courses; and second, teaching large classes is a carefully planned rhetorical endeavor—part performance, part persuasion.

Since then, the enrollment number has been pared down to 150, the room isn't quite as intimidating, and I have become extraordinarily eloquent at delivering content. However, I also have had to accept the fundamental principle of lecturing, which is just because I say it out loud does not mean students learn it. To learn, they must discover. To discover, they must internalize. To internalize, they must connect. In teaching literature that means each student must somehow connect with a particular character, a situation a character is in, or a decision a character makes. First, however, students must be willing to read. That's where the course redesign process begins.

UNT centered its Quality Enhancement Plan (QEP; see http://qep.unt .edu) around course redesign in an effort to achieve two primary goals: improve student learning outcomes in large-enrollment undergraduate courses and achieve a university-wide impact through the establishment of a community of practice and the creation of a body of redesigned courses that are sustainable and replicable. The process involves four to six faculty teams that each redesign a large-enrollment undergraduate course during a 2-year commitment period, which includes attending retreats, monthly meetings with the other teams of faculty and staff, and institution-wide forums. The course redesign takes place in this interdisciplinary community of practice. The result has been the formation of a body of next generation (NextGen) courses that use experiential and problem-based learning and encourage high levels of student engagement (Turner & Carriveau, 2010). As a result of this process, UNT now offers 20 NextGen courses, with more currently being redesigned (UNT, 2011). Each redesign team takes its own unique approach.

My approach to the redesign of a literature course is to combine the best practices of traditional pedagogical methodology of literary analysis with the advantages that technology has to offer. The idea is not to replace the content; in fact, the redesigned course materials supplement a traditional textbook (*Norton Anthology of World Literature*). Instead, I use technology to move students through a process of internalizing—not memorizing—the material, of experiencing the literature by interacting with it and by relating it to their own lives and experiences. In combining tradition with technology, I aim to overcome some of the problems of the traditional large-enrollment lecture course.

World Literature is a core curriculum humanities course with an annual enrollment of about 550 students who are taught by multiple instructors in multiple sections ranging from 35 to 150 students. As one might expect, the problems are predictable at the classroom level and the departmental level: poor student attendance; poor student preparation; high drop, failure, and withdrawal rates; problems of course drift; inconsistent learning experiences; and inefficient use of faculty effort in course delivery. In short, classes like these do not meet university or departmental objectives, and they certainly do not meet the needs and objectives of students.

The goal, then, is to transform large-enrollment courses from lecture-based to student-centered learning, using cognitively rich learning activities to move students from low-level learning objectives (literal and factual learning) to medium-level objectives that require interpretive and inferential work, and toward developing high-level learning skills. The components of active learning include not only exposure to information and ideas but also experience with them through reflective dialogue. Delivery in a blended course means students practice the material online and then meet in smaller groups for interactive discussions. For example, a blended course contains more small-group discussions and fewer large lectures; the students are actively engaged in online course work using easy-to-reference online materials; and the incorporated activities require experiential and engaged learning. All efforts work toward increasing the students' higher-level learning skills and improving their success rates in the course.

Ultimately, of course, the overall objective of a course redesign is to improve student learning outcomes. The course redesign of World Literature uses Krathwohl's (2002) "A Revision of Bloom's Taxonomy of Educational Objectives" to ensure overarching fundamentals: Objectives, lessons, and assessments are aligned; learning activities include active learning components; and lessons are cognitively rich. By cognitively rich, I mean that students experience learning in all three cognitive categories: low—at the literal and factual level, where students build the essential foundational knowledge of the discipline by being asked to recall, recognize, and identify; medium—at the conceptual and procedural level, where students use their factual knowledge to begin interpretive and inferential work by being asked to apply, analyze, and interpret; and high—at the metacognitive level of knowledge, where students begin to evaluate, construct, and create. And, yes, I'm still talking about sophomore-level university work in a large-enrollment course.

COURSE STRUCTURE

How is my redesigned blended literature course structured, and how does it function differently from a traditional lecture course? In the blended World Literature courses, students meet face-to-face about 15 times per semester in six large-group lectures, for three major exams, and in six small-group discussions. In each lecture, the instructor introduces three texts from the period and focuses on one. Usually two shorter works are paired with a longer one, so students can tackle the shorter works online while rotating through group discussions of the major work. For example, grouped together are two shorter works from the Eastern tradition of the middle period— T'ang poetry (Lawall, 2002) and excerpts from *Pillow Book* (Lawall)—along with anthologized selections from *The Thousand and One Nights* (Lawall) as illustrated in the following excerpt from the syllabus:

Week 7   Lecture—Eastern Literature: *T'ang Poetry, 1001 Nights, Pillow Book*
                  Group 1: *1001 Nights* Discussion
Week 8   Group 2: *1001 Nights* Discussion
                  Group 3: *1001 Nights* Discussion

As in any lecture, the instructor introduces each work along with its historical, cultural, and literary contexts. In my course students are able to access a simple outline of the lecture notes online. In all literature courses my primary goal is to teach the principles of literary analysis while putting the various texts into their cultural context. Because the texts in World Literature and the political institutions and social practices that contributed to their creation often seem so distant from students' experiences, a second, but no less important, goal for me as a teacher is to create connections between the concepts, characters, and conflicts presented in the readings with the students' lives. Only by building relevancy between the discipline of literature and today's culture can we ensure the survival and flourishing of the field.

After the introductory lecture, each of which also models a way of approaching a text, students begin the sequence of rotating through small-group discussion sessions. In a large class of 150 students, I break the students into three groups of 50; in a medium-size class of 60–70 students, I use two groups of 30–35. Before coming to their assigned small-group discussion session, students are expected to complete the online materials relating to that text. Additionally, when not in lectures or small groups, students complete the online modules for the other two assigned texts.

In constructing my blended course, I have used technology to meet a variety of learning styles through visual, audio, and interactive content. Each of the online modules has a similar structure. A sample table of contents includes the following:

- Introduction—a brief statement of the overall approach to the particular work
- Lesson Objectives—an attainable list of expectations, each of which can be achieved by active participation in the lesson activities
- Reading Assignment—a clarification of the exact pages, sections, or excerpts assigned
- Interactive Map—a visual representation of where the literature or author originates
- Interactive Activity—an online exercise that allows students to gauge their mastery of the reading material
- Discussion Topics—a list of open-ended, interpretive questions that encourage higher-level engagement with the material and with other students
- Quiz—a formative assessment of the student's mastery at the literal factual level

The course as a whole contains lesson modules for each and every assigned reading. Each lesson begins with a set of measurable lesson objectives and progresses through online learning activities and interactions related to the readings. These online activities prepare students for small-group face-to-face meetings in which they will debate, discuss, collaborate, and make presentations on the material. Each module concludes with an assessment that measures how well students meet the stated lesson objectives. This recursive process employs technology at its most efficient and with engaging possibilities.

PEDAGOGICAL RATIONALE

The purpose of the online components pertaining to the longer readings in the course is to provide practical, interactive ways for the students to actively engage with the reading material prior to class. The online components provide a self-administered, creative, and productive way for students to gauge their own understanding and mastery of the assigned material. Once students have completed the online components, they come to small-group discussions ready to debate, make presentations, and otherwise actively participate in higher-level learning. In addition to increasing student interaction and developing higher-level learning skills, the online components of the course design also appeal to a variety of learning styles and allow for more effective use of classroom time.

The instructional strategies employed in the course promote student engagement with course content. Many of the cognitively rich online learning activities are designed to help students master the material at the literal, factual level of understanding. This dimension of knowledge lays the groundwork for increasingly higher-level learning to take place in the face-to-face meetings. In conventional large-enrollment sections of World Literature, students typically come to class not having read the material or not understanding the basic elements of genre, plot, and character. These lower-level objectives can be addressed and achieved online so that valuable class time is not spent merely summarizing. Since the course reading is cumulative, students need to do more than memorize; they must internalize the characters they encounter, the situations those characters face, and the decisions those characters make. The strategies writers use to depict characters, situations, and decisions in the ancient world will be built upon by writers of the Middle Ages and then by writers of the Renaissance. The online activities track these patterns throughout the semester. What look like games are actually sophisticated learning tasks that are masked to be approachable and obtainable for students.

For example, the Gilgamesh journey game that I created has students organize the main events in the character's life in chronological order so we can spend class time analyzing those events instead of summarizing them. Another online game is structured as a path to Confucian enlightenment, where students can also earn pearls of wisdom. This creative, visual application offers an alternative way for students to gauge their own understanding of this pithy material. In another online exercise, students spend an evening with Aristotle in a Greek theater evaluating classical elements of a tragedy, using the thumbs-up or thumbs-down gesture. Students then have to apply these Aristotelian conventions of tragedy to a Shakespearean tragedy in the Renaissance. As appropriate, lessons make available reading resouces, such as links to further introductory material about Greek theater, Greek stagecraft, and how Romans remodeled the classical Greek theater. Furthermore, students use recent, reliable, and relevant links to interactive versions of Dante's *Inferno* to locate characters and mythological figures from Dante's work and from previous works they have read (such as Virgil's *Aeneid*). Many of these same characters, figures, and places reappear in the Renaissance epic *Paradise Lost*.

In developing these types of learning objects, I think we all have to face a legitimate and compelling question: Will the students actually use the interactive learning objects that are designed and incorporated into the lessons? Certainly, some students skim past learning opportunities, especially ungraded ones. It seems to me that one's approach to creating and designing learning objects requires balance. First, the design efforts must be geared primarily toward integrating the information into the very means students experience the material, making them an essential—not ancillary—way to work through the content. In addition, learning objects must be a nonthreatening method for the students to measure their mastery of the material on an ongoing, incremental basis. These two methods of developing technology can ensure greater success for students in a blended course, and they ensure that the students are taking greater responsibility in the learning process and in the outcome.

INTERACTION AND COLLABORATION

After students have completed the online activities that help them master the material at the literal, factual level, they move to the second step in the learning process—small-group discussions. Interaction and collaboration can take many forms in a blended environment, including learner to learner, learner to content, and learner to instructor. To encourage interaction and collaboration, then, discussion topics are included in the development of each of the reading lessons or modules. Instructors can selectively release and use these discussion topics in three ways: as the basis of small-group, face-to-face discussions; as topic ideas for compositions; or as topics for online discussion postings. The purpose of the collaborative tools in World Literature is to stimulate class discussion and to encourage feedback and insights from engaging with others.

In my redesigned courses, students are expected to post comments on an online discussion board for lessons that have no scheduled face-to-face meeting. Using the excerpt from the sample syllabus on page 89, if the class is scheduled to meet face-to-face to discuss *A Thousand and One Nights* (Lawall, 2002) but work through *T'ang* poetry (Lawall) and the selections of the *Pillow Book* (Lawall) using online materials, then part of the online work for those two modules includes a discussion posting assignment. Five topics are available for each lesson so that 10 students from each group of 50 (or 6–7 students from a group of 30–35) will post comments on each question. Discussion postings require original thoughts and complete answers to specific questions. In general students must post a reply to an initial question as well as respond to two classmates' postings. Academic assistants grade the discussion postings for their set group of 50 students all semester based on the rubric in Table 4.1.

In grading the first few rounds of discussion postings, I was admittedly disappointed. Certainly they are not as developed as writing composition assignments in which students must write a traditional 250–300-word analytical interpretation. Then, as my teaching assistants pointed out, I realized that even the students whose discussion postings were the most lacking were still participating. Had those students been in a face-to-face setting, they probably would not have spoken at all. And when the face-to-face discussions are structured as small groups of students that had already been interacting in online discussions and are choreographed to include everyone, then the participation is greater and the level of learning is higher.

A set of online discussion questions in a blended World Literature course might look like the one in Figure 4.1 from Dante's *Divine Comedy*.

As is the pedagogical philosophy behind the entire course redesign, even the set of *Divine Comedy* discussion questions blends the traditional approach with technology. For example, question number 2 requires that students first match the inhabitants of the *Inferno* with a quoted description

Table 4.1   Rubric for Evaluating Online Discussion Posts (50 points)

This interaction is used to stimulate class discussion and to encourage feedback and insight from engaging in synergy with others. Your participation in the discussion will be evaluated based on this rubric at midterm and at the end of the semester. Your score is dependent on the quality of your contribution, not just the number of posts.

Criteria	Needs Improvement 1–5 points	Meets Expectations 5–15 points	Excellent 10–20 points
Quality of Content	• No addition of useful ideas but a repetition of others' views • Personal experiences are stated but not related to topic • Strays from topic to easier topics requiring no reading • Viewpoints are not substantiated by textual examples	• Adds some useful ideas to the group process • Contribution based more on relationship (e.g., "I agree with you" or "You did great!") without much substantive cognitive contribution • Digresses from topic but returned to it	• Substantive presentation of critical and useful ideas presented in a logical manner • Cognitively stimulating or challenging • Textual examples are referenced and related to topic • Stays with topic; not sidetracked
Attitude Toward Participation	• A negative attitude reflected through minimal participation, less than substantive posts, being less open to others' ideas, and providing little or no original explanation	• Attitude reflects that participation is more to fulfill requirement than a real interest • Appears less eager to challenge the views of participants to maintain interest in the discussion • Late to join the discussion	• Positive general attitude—works to advance the group conversation • Encourages others to participate by posing additional questions related to the topic or reading • Receptive to differing viewpoints, allowing the group to explore all members' perspectives
Effort Input	• Not well prepared for discussion within timeline • Needs encouragement from others on ideas to enhance participation • Contributes minimally	• Participation in chunks instead of spread out consistently throughout the discussion	• Starts group discussion right away • Does fair share of the work or takes responsibility for enhancing discussion • Contribution consistent and spread out

from the text through a drag-and-drop exercise. Also, important concepts and terms, such as *contrapasso*, or *counterpenalty*, are linked to an online glossary so students can click on the term and get a pop-up definition or explanation. These features may sound simple; however, they are carefully incorporated so students have various ways of interacting with and thereby mastering the material.

Figure 4.1 Divine Comedy Discussion Topics

Divine Comedy Discussion Topics

Use the following topics to prepare for small-group discussion and as the basis of a reading composition.

1. Explain how Dante can be classified as an absolutist and how Boccaccio can be classified as a relativist. Define each term and give examples from each work.

2. Match the following inhabitants of the Inferno with their contrapasso. Define what is morally meant by contrapasso, interpret the following specific examples, and briefly explain the significance of each. In other words, how is the punishment of sin the sin itself, not retribution?

Match the following inhabitants of the Inferno with their contrapasso.

Those who "are damned because they sinned within the flesh, subjecting reason to the rule of lust"

Those who "lacked baptism" or who "lived before Christianity"

"For these defects, and for no other evil, we are now lost and punished just with this: we have no hope and yet we live in longing."

The Gluttonous

The Greedy and the Wasteful

Correct!

3. In Dante's *The Divine Comedy*, the Pilgrim is warned against "cowardice" several times in the opening canto of the *Inferno*. What is meant by the term cowardice? What figures exemplify cowardice? How is the Pilgrim to arm himself against cowardice?

4. Numerous literary works from Medieval Europe reveal an awareness of the need for reform in the Catholic Church. Discuss 3 instances of criticism of the Church from any of the representative works from the Middle period.

5. Compare and contrast the experience of Francesca and Paolo as described in Canto 5 of the *Inferno* with that of Statius in Cantos 21-22 of *Purgatorio*. What does the Pilgrim learn from each of these figures—about the power of literature? About choosing what one reads? About the need for correct interpretation?

All course materials © 2007, Dr T.M. Gau

Furthermore, to promote higher-level learning, many of the discussion questions in this exercise demand that students put what they read into the context of other readings: Question number 1 asks students to compare the classification of Boccaccio as a relativist to Dante as an absolutist; number 4 invites students to see this work in the context of others of the period that criticize the Catholic church; and number 5 requires that students compare characters from the *Inferno* with one from *Purgatorio*. Discussion assignments like these move students from low-level learning objectives (literal and factual learning) into medium-level objectives that require interpretive and inferential work.

Another way the redesign improves student learning is by making options available that do not exist in a traditional large classroom setting. Development of the online learning activities and interactions should be guided by the material itself: What pedagogical approach most facilitates student engagement—at a higher level this time—with that particular reading? In the poetry sections of early and middle Chinese literature, for example, students can hear the poems read in Chinese and English, as well as read the poems in the textbook. As students prepare to write an interpretive discussion posting on a particular poem, they can click on a link to hear the poem read by a native Chinese speaker.

Discussion postings can also move from the medium or interpretive level of learning into the metacognitive level in which students not only analyze but begin to create. For example, after having read excerpts from the *Pillow Book* (Lawall, 2002) by female Japanese author Sei Shonagon from the middle period, students are asked to take one of the categories of Shonagon's passages—such as "Depressing Things," "Hateful Things," "Elegant Things," "Unsuitable Things," "Embarrassing Things," "Awkward Things," or "Pleasing Things"—and modernize it. Their entry for the discussion forum requires they mimic Shonagon's highly refined sense of taste and aestheticism as they develop a contemporary entry under one of those particular categories. Being able to create is a hallmark of critical thinking and a shared, fundamental objective in university-level courses.

Technology can also be used as an aid in face-to-face discussions. Referring to Week 7 on the sample syllabus on p. 89, the students attend a lecture on representative Eastern works of the middle period as a large group. Individually and online, the class reads, listens to, and posts comments in a discussion on T'ang poetry, then works through the *Pillow Book* (Lawall, 2002) reading and posts a creative entry in a modernized version. Meanwhile, they are scheduled to rotate through discussion sessions on *A Thousand and One Nights* (Lawall). At this point in the course, I release the online graphic of the stories (see Figure 4.2) that explains visually a complicated, layered storytelling format often used by writers of the middle period.

Once students can envision who the narrator of a particular story is, they can more easily see the relationships and the parallels between the narrator's situation and the storyteller's. In classroom discussion sessions, students share the connections they make and begin the process of analyzing and interpreting.

Other types of collaborative learning take place in the face-to-face, small-group meetings where students team up, debate, and present their own conclusions in the context of other comments. One of my most successful assignments is the Authorship Debate that precedes the reading of a Shakespearean play. This assignment requires students to read about a current controversy: Who is the author of Shakespeare's plays? They read current articles, each of which builds a case for a particular candidate. When the

Figure 4.2   Narrators of the Prologue to *The Thousand and One Nights*

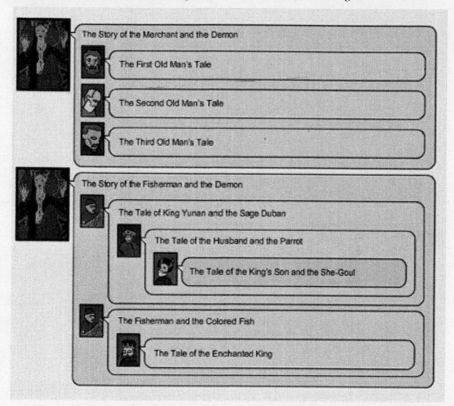

students come to small-group discussion, they are randomly assigned a candidate they must present evidence for and defend from objections as the author of the plays. The stage is set for a real, live debate with informed and active participants. After the debate, students are asked to abandon their assigned roles and discuss the conclusions they have reached through the process. The Authorship Debate assignment has proved so successful in the sophomore-level World Literature course that now I use it as the opening activity of my senior-level Shakespeare course to promote preparation, engagement, and relevancy from the beginning of the semester.

This type of collaborative debate does not require students to meet outside class; instead, it sets the expectation that coming to class prepared is not only essential, it is also exciting, relevant, and worthwhile. One danger of the blended learning environment is that students may adopt the attitude that they don't need to come to class. Therefore, face-to-face time must be readily applicable and germane—to the course and to student lives and experiences.

Furthermore, interactive and collaborative activities like these provide tangible, even measurable, evidence of engagement at higher levels of learning.

Collaborative learning is an integral part of studying literature. Students often learn as much from one another as they do from a well-informed, articulate instructor. Therefore, this redesigned course includes components of lecture and discussion in online and face-to-face formats. In lecture students receive an integrated overview of a text's historical, cultural, and literary contexts. Online, students are engaged in discussion postings, which help them prepare for or reflect on face-to-face meetings. Combined, these activities move the students from the lower-level stage of learning factual and literal information to the medium and high levels of cognitive complexity that involve analyzing, interpreting, evaluating, and synthesizing representative texts from the Eastern and Western traditions and relating them to their literary and cultural contexts.

ASSESSMENT

The assessment strategies for this course were created in the context of the QEP (http://qep.unt.edu) and selected in collaboration with the assessments specialist in the Center for Learning Enhancement, Assessment, and Redesign (CLEAR; http://clear.unt.edu/). The redesign of the World Literature course is based on the recursive relationship between student learning outcomes (SLOs), the activities and exercises that allow students to practice those outcomes, and the various forms of assessment used to measure proficiency and achievement. Assessment allows professors, staff, and faculty of departments and universities to make valid inferences about our students and our programs. It provides evidence of and makes us accountable for doing our jobs in developing student talents and abilities, and it can help us evaluate the degree to which students are engaged in the learning cycle.

I used to think assessment was the final component of a course. Through the course redesign process, however, I have learned that assessments are inextricably tied to course outcomes. First and foremost, those outcome statements we write at the beginning of every semester for every course must be measurable. Again, to develop specific measurable outcomes for the World Literature courses, I used Anderson et al.'s (2001) *A Taxonomy for Learning, Teaching, and Assessing* to ensure that outcomes, lessons, and assessments are aligned. From the very beginning of the course, the syllabus describes how this blended class uses various online and face-to-face activities to achieve the primary course goals and the SLOs:

COURSE DESCRIPTION

Combining tradition with technology in a blended format (partially online, partially face-to-face), students encounter some of the greatest works of ancient, medieval, and Renaissance world literature. Classes meet in large and small face-to-face groups. In addition, interactive online activities, debates, and self-assessment exercises encourage students to experience—not just read about—the literature and to apply its lessons to their own lives. The course learning goals are that students will be able to do the following:

1. Demonstrate awareness and recognition of the scope and variety of works of literature.
2. Read critically and analytically.
3. Construct informed, organized, and coherent written responses to literary texts in a variety of rhetorical modes.
4. Actively discuss ideas with others.

To achieve these goals, students practice the following tasks:

1. Recall and recognize the historical sequence of major literary figures, texts, and movements in the ancient, medieval, and Renaissance periods.
2. Identify conventional literary genres, elements, and devices.
3. Employ discipline-specific vocabulary to analyze the relationship between form and content.
4. Relate literary concepts, principles, terms, strategies, and styles to a range of literature.
5. Analyze, evaluate, and interpret representative texts from the Eastern and Western traditions and relate them to their literary and cultural contexts.
6. Compare and contrast major literary figures, their situations, and their decisions.
7. Make connections among various periods, texts, authors, and characters.
8. Evaluate the ideas presented in a text, their implications, and their relationship to ideas beyond the text.

Being confronted with a tangible, attainable, and concise list of expectations encourages a student's commitment to the course at the outset. In her article, "Making the Grade," Marilyn M. Lombardi (2008) argues that undergraduates have begun to view themselves as "learning consumers" with expectations to be met in their education. Not only do learners want to know the criteria by which they will be judged, but they also want processes in place to help them improve and develop, guided by clear, practical, and specific feedback. These "consumer learners" are demanding increased transparency from instructors. They want to be let in on the instructor's thinking process, asking why the course was designed in this fashion, what the instructor is trying to accomplish, why the learning activities are relevant, and what the criteria are for judging student success. (p. 4)

Many different instruments are available to assess the SLOs—multiple-choice items (for formative and summative assessment), constructed response items (an umbrella term for all assessment items requiring writing, such as short-answer or extended essays), and course surveys. Likewise, each of these must be measured with reliability and validity.

Assessment focuses on the evaluation of student work toward the achievement of measurable learning outcomes. In effect, these instruments of assessments are actually another means to improve student learning.

I began the redesign process by creating a course blueprint or assessment plan (see Table 4.2). For World Literature, I developed a three-tiered structure that aligns outcomes and assessments beginning with the large course goals down to the specific lesson outcomes for each major learning module. The three tiers are institutional, departmental, and classroom, which are based on Ronald S. Carriveau's (2010) "Applying a Three-Level Model" in developing student learning outcomes. The overall course goals at the institutional level set the standard for academic effectiveness; in other words, the four overarching primary outcomes for World Literature meet university standards and expectations for students taking a World Literature course at UNT. The departmental level or general outcomes then provide a strategic plan for accomplishing each of those overarching course goals; in other words, the outcomes at the departmental level indicate how students can achieve the course goals when taking a World Literature course in the Department of English at UNT. Finally, the classroom or specific outcomes are the pedagogical arena where students demonstrate how successful they have been in meeting the expectations set; by meeting these classroom outcomes, a student taking Gau's World Literature course in the Department of English at UNT effectively meets the expectations of the lesson, the department, and the institution.

In addition to outlining the goals and SLOs, the course assessment plan shows the types of assessment instruments used to measure each outcome.

Table 4.2 Assessment Plan for N-Gen ENGL2210: World Literature I

This table shows the alignment of student learning outcomes at the institutional, departmental, and course levels. The column on the right indicates the number of test items for each outcome, and categorizes them by cognitive level: Low (literal and factual), Med (medium: interpretive and analytical), and Hi (high: metacognitive).

Institutional Level Course Learning Goals	Departmental Level General Student Learning Outcomes	Classroom Level Specific Lesson Learning Outcomes	No. test items by cognitive level				
			Low	Med	Hi	Tot	CR*
1. Demonstrate an awareness and recognition of the scope and variety of works of literature	1.1 Recall and recognize the historical sequence of major literary figures, texts, and movements within the Ancient, Middle, and Renaissance periods	Recognize that the history of representative epics are oral or written compositions	6	2		8	
	1.2 Identify conventional literary genres, elements, and devices	Identify major characters and figures that appear in more than one text	6	2		8	
	1.3 Employ discipline specific vocabulary in order to analyze the relationship between form and content	Apply genre characteristics to representative texts	4	4		8	1
	1.4 Relate literary or cultural concepts, principles, terms, strategies, and styles to a range of literature	Identify and connect literary or cultural concepts as they directly relate to representative texts	5	3		8	
2. Read critically and analytically	2.1 Analyze, evaluate, interpret, and synthesize representative texts from the Eastern and Western traditions and relate them to their literary and cultural contexts	Relate cultural qualities of a hero to a representative character	3	2	2	7	1
	2.2 Compare and contrast major literary figures, their situations, and their decisions	Compare the Eastern depiction of fate, virtue, and heroism to the Western depiction in representative texts	2	3	2	7	1
	2.3 Make connections among various periods, texts, authors, and characters	Differentiate between concepts, such as absolutism and relativism, using examples from representative texts	3	2	2	7	1
	2.4 Evaluate the ideas presented in a text, their implications, and their relationship to ideas beyond the text	Evaluate characters' decisions and actions in the context of their various cultures and worldviews	2	2	3	7	1

Table 4.2 (Continued)

Institutional Level Course Learning Goals	Departmental Level General Student Learning Outcomes	Classroom Level Specific Lesson Learning Outcomes	No. test items by cognitive level				
			Low	Med	Hi	Tot	CR*
3. Construct informed, organized, and coherent written responses to literary texts	3.1 Formulate a central interpretive idea about the texts						
	3.2 Develop ideas logically and coherently with adequate supporting textual examples	Written composition (See Constructed Response Grading Rubric, Table 4.3)					
	3.3 Present ideas clearly and concisely						
	3.4 Observe the standard conventions of formatting, citation, grammar, and punctuation						
4. Actively discuss ideas with others	4.1 Present (in discussion posts or small groups) information or conclusions that help other students summarize, synthesize, and integrate the conceptual material	Relate readings to life and academic experiences					
	4.2 Establish a relevancy between literature and how it affects one's life, personal values, ethical behavior, aesthetic judgment, and problem solving	Make interdisciplinary connections, such as with history, philosophy, art, rhetoric, business, politics					
		Total exam items	31	20	9	**60**	5

*CR (constructed response) items are all at the medium and high cognitive levels.

The first two course learning goals—to demonstrate an awareness and recognition of the scope and variety of works of literature and to read critically and analytically—are measured through the three unit exams. Each of these in-class unit exams consists of 60 multiple-choice items and 5 constructed response items. The multiple-choice items on these summative exams vary in difficulty level, including each of the learning levels—low (literal and factual), medium (interpretive and analytical), and high (metacognitive). The five constructed response items provide a complementary measure of student achievement of the first two course learning goals. These five short-answer items are all in the difficulty range of medium to high, since constructed response is still one of the best means of meaningfully measuring students' ability to master and apply concepts in authentic contexts.

Overall, then, this course uses four main types of assessment strategies to measure student learning outcomes: formative, summative, constructed response, and surveys. Each of these assessment tools begins with and is founded upon measurable learning objectives. The course blueprint outlines three levels of objectives—institutional, departmental, and classroom—to ensure the reciprocity of the objectives from the macro- to the microlevels. On the microlevel, each lesson begins with a set of lesson outcomes, each outcome has an activity that allows the student to practice achieving that outcome, and each outcome is assessed using one or more of these instruments.

FORMATIVE ASSESSMENT

One of the most effective ways to improve student learning in blended courses is low-stakes mastery quizzes and games that allow students to self-assess how well they are mastering the material at the literal and conceptual levels. Formative assessments in my course include online quizzes and activities. Each lesson module concludes with an online quiz that emphasizes the assigned reading at the literal, factual level of learning. I specify that each quiz can be taken up to three times for the highest score, providing students with ample opportunity to demonstrate mastery of the material before going on to higher-level learning activities such as discussions. Of course, some instructors are not yet comfortable administering tests online. My strategy is to differentiate quiz questions from exam questions and to use quizzes as a foundation for more difficult questions on the summative exams. For example, if a student can answer this low-level question about the plot of the *Iliad* on a quiz (asterisk indicates the correct response):

Why does Zeus initially agree to help the Trojans in the war?
A. As a favor to Thetis who asks on behalf of her son*
B. To revenge the death of his son Sarpedon
C. To spite his wife, Hera

then that student can use that factual knowledge to answer a medium-level, conceptual item such as this on the unit summative exam:

What element in Greek literature does the following passage represent?
"And crouching down at his feet, quickly grasping his knees with her left hand, her right hand holding him underneath the chin, she prayed to the lord god Zeus, the son of Cronus: 'Zeus, Father Zeus! If ever I served you well . . .'"
A. Invocation of the muse
B. Divine intervention
C. Supplication*

In addition to an online multiple-choice quiz with literal and factual items, each reading module includes a game or online interaction that allows students to practice meeting the SLOs and to gauge their own level of mastery of the material. In a visually enhanced bingo-style online exercise, for example, students review concepts, characters, and cultural elements from the Renaissance period and the ancient world that helped to shape early modern texts. This activity requires the application of new and previously studied concepts to the current texts. Students find it challenging to recall ancient and medieval figures they have encountered, such as Achilles, Dido, Cicero, and Dante, while tracing concepts that have been redefined through the periods, such as moderation, fortune, virtue, and then actively apply them to the Renaissance texts they are studying. These formative quizzes and activities are designed to serve as preparatory springboards for more difficult items on the summative exams. In fact, my students use the multiple-choice quizzes and games to prepare for the exams.

SUMMATIVE ASSESSMENT: MULTIPLE CHOICE

My goal in the redesigned class is to incorporate higher-cognitive-level items into a multiple-choice test, which offers a high degree of reliability and validity, thereby moving its traditional use as a low-level assessment tool to a higher-level learning tool. This tool can provide valid information so instructors can reliably draw inferences about students' critical thinking ability.

Of course using a multiple-choice format is controversial, especially in the humanities. However, multiple-choice questions can be used to assess a student's knowledge of material in varying degrees of higher-level thinking. Developing specific test items that address the three levels of learning involves a process of gathering item analysis data and analyzing statistics and then using that research to make evaluation and redesign decisions, which can include changes to the curriculum and design of the course. There is thus a direct and concrete relationship between assessment analysis and redesign—from the micro- to the macrolevels.

Using the multiple-choice format does not mean, however, that I have completely replaced the constructed response assessment tool. In fact, I think the difficulty levels of items on the multiple-choice tests will correlate with the rubric used to measure constructed responses (essays and compositions). Put together, these assessment tools that form the blueprint for the course will provide reliable and valid information for making redesign decisions that will increase student learning.

The three major exams on the three main literary periods (ancient, medieval, Renaissance) are summative assessments. Each exam includes 60 multiple-choice items that are explicitly connected to an institutional, departmental, or classroom outcome, and each item is ranked according to difficulty level (low, medium, high) depending on the level of cognitive complexity required. Furthermore, each unit exam also includes five short-answer constructed response items that likewise meet the objectives and are graded on a rubric provided for the academic assistants. These concept-oriented questions often originate from the discussion topics covered in the assigned lessons. The measurable objectives at these three levels become the basis for creating actual test items. These test items in turn measure the three main cognitive categories of learning: low (literal and factual), medium (interpretive and inferential), and high (evaluative and critical thinking).

SUMMATIVE ASSESSMENT: CONSTRUCTED RESPONSE

While multiple-choice items can show learning has occurred, writing can allow students to express the way their thinking has changed. Savory, Burnett, and Goodburn (2007) classify this type of written assessment as "delayed," as it "measures learning or growth after students have had time to reflect on or study the issue or course material. They are more formal, require more preparation from both teacher and student, and yield documented results" (p. 65). The combination of quantitative and qualitative assessment methods provides multiple forms of feedback regarding the students' mastery of the material.

In addition to writing constructed response answers on exams, students are also required to write 500- to 600-word compositions throughout the course. The rubric used to evaluate and provide feedback on these papers includes the standard rhetorical elements of thesis, evidence, and organization, but it also adds the element of significance. Students in this course are encouraged to relate to the characters, situations, and decisions they encounter in the literature. In their papers, they must show how what they read is relevant to their own lives. The rubric shown in Table 4.3 and a sample composition, with rollover interactions or information that pops up when the mouse crosses over, are made available to the students via the home page of the course.

SURVEY ASSESSMENT

A final kind of delayed assessment in the redesigned course is the use of surveys. Three student surveys are used to encourage critical reflection and analysis of course content and format and to measure student attitudes, perceptions, appreciation, and competency:

1. Survey of Student Attitude Toward Subject
2. Survey of Student Perceptions About Literature
3. Survey of Student Preference: Redesigned Versus Face-to-Face Format

The Survey of Student Attitude Toward Subject is administered at the beginning and end of the course. This survey compares student attitudes toward the subject matter when beginning the course with attitudes when finishing the course. Validated by the SouthCentral Instrument Library and Data Repository, this survey provides an opportunity for students to give measurable feedback about the course. The information from the survey is used to better understand the relationships between student attitudes toward the subject and the effectiveness of the course delivery format. For the spring 2008 semester, a statistically significant difference (.05) between pre- and postcourse responses was found on these positively worded questions, indicating an increase in the following positive opinions toward the course:

+ .33   I like this subject
+ .36   Knowing this subject makes me more employable
+ .23   This subject should be required for all students
+ .54   I know a lot about this subject
+ .33   This subject is relevant to my personal goals

Table 4.3 Constructed Response Grading Rubric

Dimension	5	10	15	20	Total
THESIS A debatable, problematic assertion	An attempt at an assertion is made, but it is not problematic; discussion is mostly summary	Assertion is obvious and contributes little to the ongoing discussion	Assertion is interpretive and moderately contributes to the ongoing discussion	Assertion is interpretive, problematic and clearly contributes to the ongoing discussion	
EVIDENCE Substantiate the assertion	Relationship between the examples and the assertion is unclear	Examples merely summarize or are not clearly or consistently linked to the assertion	Examples moderately support and are relevant to the assertion	Examples clearly support and are relevant to the assertion	
ORGANIZATION Coherent structure	Logical assertion is weak; little consistency in supporting statements; and/or no transitions	Assertion is logically maintained to a moderate degree; supporting statements are weak; few transitions	Assertion is logically maintained; supporting statements are moderately consistent; moderate use of transitions	Assertion is logically maintained throughout; supporting statements are highly consistent; excellent use of transitions	

Table 4.3 (Continued)

SIGNIFICANCE Establish a relevancy	Conclusion merely summarizes the assertion attempt	Significance or relevancy is implied but not clearly conveyed	Conclusion moderately conveys the significance or relevancy of the assertion	Conclusion clearly conveys the significance or relevancy of the assertion	Total
Mechanics	0	5	10		
Grammar, sentence structure, punctuation	Proofreading errors are clearly evident	Inaccuracies make paper moderately difficult to read	Few inaccuracies, advanced vocabulary, deliberate word choice	N/A	
Quotations	Inaccurately cited or integrated	Accurately cited and integrated	N/A	N/A	
Format	Does not meet MLA standards: format, heading, spacing, margins, and title	Meets MLA standards: format, heading, spacing, margins, and title	N/A	N/A	

Grand Total _____

Feedback:

Similarly, a statistically significant difference between pre- and post-course responses was found on these negatively worded questions, indicating that the following negative opinions toward the course were reduced:

−.23   This is a difficult subject for me
−.49   Learning this subject requires a lot of hard work
−.29   This subject is difficult to understand
−.42   I am scared by this subject

Any professor of English would find it rewarding to know students find the study of literature useful, relevant, and worthwhile.

The Survey of Student Perceptions About Literature, administered at the end of the semester, is designed to gather information about student perceptions on how much they improved or increased their skills in three main areas: competency, critical and evaluative thinking, and appreciation of literature. The final five questions of the survey address instructional design. Students were asked to indicate the degree to which certain course experiences were beneficial to their learning using the same 4-point scale: 1 = *very little*; 2 = *somewhat*; 3 = *a good deal*; 4 = *a great deal*. The most positive results were obtained in the section on the instructional design of the redesigned course:

- The blended learning format for this course helped with my personal scheduling needs.
- The online exercises aided in my learning the material.
- The small group discussions aided in my understanding of the material.
- Maintaining the same group increased my ability to participate in online and class discussions.
- The blended learning format helped me to succeed in this class.

Students rated each of these aspects as having influenced their success in the course "a good deal." The exception is the penultimate item, which asks about maintaining the same group. According to this survey, students believe the smaller group size contributes more to their learning than having the same members in that group.

Interpreted together, the perception surveys demonstrate that when students are presented with opportunities to master the content at the literal and factual level in an online environment, their fears (of difficulty, applicability, usefulness) are decreased. Furthermore, students perceive they are better prepared to engage in higher-level critical thinking activities, and they more readily see the relevance of the material to personal and professional goals.

A final survey administered during the last month of the semester asks students about their preference for course format—redesigned (blended) versus face-to-face (traditional)—using the following question: If you were to start this course over again, would you prefer a traditional face-to-face format, or would you prefer the N-Gen redesign format you are experiencing? Please tell why.

The results show that a significantly higher percentage of students (70%) preferred a redesigned course format versus a traditional face-to-face course format (30%), irrespective of their final grades in the course.

Student comments on why they preferred the redesigned blended format versus a traditional face-to-face format were categorized by the primary reasons for the student's choice. Four categories emerged for the redesigned format and four for the face-to-face format. For the redesigned course format, the reasons fell into the following categories:

1. Pace (liked that they could control the rate at which they absorbed information)
2. Flexibility (liked that they could do assignments whenever and wherever they wanted)
3. Learning (found it easier to learn content when it is Internet-based)
4. Practice (more opportunities to practice and learn)

For the traditional face-to-face course format, the reasons fell into the following categories:

1. Manage (the need for structure to not procrastinate)
2. Learning (found it easier to learn content when format is face-to-face)
3. People (a preference for face-to-face interactions)
4. Technical (difficulties with computers, network, and technology used)

Table 4.4 shows a typical comment for each of the reason categories for the format preference of redesigned versus face-to-face, and the number of comments per category. There are 128 comments from students who prefer the redesigned blended format and 44 comments from students who prefer face-to-face format, for a total of 172 comments. The total number of comments collected is 182. Most of the nonincluded remaining 10 comments

Table 4.4 Typical Student Comments for Choosing Redesigned Versus Face-to-Face Course Formats

Format	Reason Category (n)	Typical Comment
Redesign	Pace (6)	I liked that I could do most of the work at my own pace when I had time to do it. If I wanted to go a little slower, I could.
	Flexibility (58)	This course allowed me to work out my hectic schedule. Being able to submit quizzes and stuff online made my life easier.
	Learning (58)	I like to learn from a bunch of different sources at once and this course really allowed me the chance to do that. You got stuff from online sources and you got some face-to-face interaction and I think I ended up learning more in this course than I would have otherwise.
	Practice (6)	I always liked the fact that you could go back and take the quizzes over and over again until you got them right. I really feel like that helped me a lot in the class.
Face-to-face	Manage (10)	I prefer a traditional face-to-face lecture because I would often forget about online assignments and I think my grade suffered. I need more structure in my courses, so I need to come to campus more often!
	Learning (19)	I seem to absorb the information better in a traditional class format when I'm taking notes during a lecture. It just suits my learning style better.
	People (10)	I can't seem to learn without a teacher lecturing to me and me taking notes. Maybe it's something about the interaction in the communication. I guess I just like being around people.
	Technical (5)	I don't trust submitting my quizzes online. The internet didn't seem to be reliable. Sometimes the website would be slow or wouldn't work at all. SO frustrating!

combined so much information it was not possible to assign the comment to one specific category.

SUCCESS RATES BASED ON GRADES

Student perceptions as revealed in the survey and comment data are also verified by the success rates based on grades. Success is defined as a grade of A, B, or C. Over the past 3 years, my two conventional large-enrollment sections of World Literature I courses averaged a success rate of 67%. For the first implementation semester of the redesigned course in fall 2007, the success rate was 71% across sections 001 and 002 of the course, an increase of 4%. At the end of the second implementation semester in spring 2008, the success rate increased to 84%. A 10% increase may indicate a more effective use of resources—for students, instructors, and the university. The increased success rates of the two redesigned course sections may also indicate that the strategies of moving toward experiential, student-centered, and active learning that emphasize analysis, synthesis, and application are having a significantly positive impact on student learning.

It is notable that higher-level cognitive items are included in the summative assessment vehicles in the redesigned sections. These items are written to match the intent of the redesigned student learning outcome statements. Previous course administrations did not include these higher-level outcomes and items.

Overall, the assessment results show the blended course design addresses the problems of poor attitude, lack of preparation, low success rates, and low-level passive learning through memorization, and transforms the classroom into a discovery-based, student-led place of active and experiential learning built around interaction with the primary materials.

LEARNER SUPPORT

The final area to consider when redesigning a course is learner support, the resources made available to students. A standard form of support to include are links to university resources. These institutional resources complement course-specific manuals. From the home page, students can link to student resources for technical support and training offered through the university. Students can also link to the computing help desk, the UNT library, and Distributed Learning Services, as well as obtain e-mail, phone, and in-person assistance. Students can access the library catalog, the Ask-a-Librarian Reference Service, and can search for electronic resources such as e-books and e-journals. Another form of learner support is the incorporation of Supplemental Instruction, one of the programs offered by the UNT Learning Center. An undergraduate student who has successfully completed this World Literature I course provides regularly scheduled, out-of-class, group study sessions 3 times each week. From the home page, information about the Supplemental Instruction leader, his or her contact information, and the weekly scheduled sessions are available to students.

Two customized online guides are provided in the redesigned World Literature I course—one for students and one for instructors. Both are available online and were created and updated by UNT students in a senior-level technical writing class. Both guides provide a basic overview of Blackboard as it relates specifically to the course, the course home page and contents, and the tools available and in use for the World Literature I course.

The student guide for the blended section of World Literature I clearly, concisely, and completely explains how technology can be accessed and used by students for all assignments, activities, and interactions in the course. This course-specific learner orientation complements the university's own resources for students, which can also be accessed directly through the home page of the course.

The online student guide provides an accessible reference tool for the students regardless of their levels of technological expertise. Students can proceed directly to the individual section they need to reference. After the introduction to Blackboard, the student guide is divided into four main sections: Course Content Tools (including syllabus, assignments, assessments, and media library), Communication Tools (mail, calendar, announcements, discussions, chat and whiteboard, who's online), Evaluation Tools (my grades, my progress), and Helpful Tools and Resources (notes, my files, search, help). Each section of the manual is complete with screenshots, icons, and clear, easy-to-follow, step-by-step instructions.

CONCLUSION

Courses such as the one described here increase the quality of a department's offerings while providing a basic framework that meets university, departmental, and course objectives. Offering an alternative-style course does not cost any more and uses less classroom space. In a well-redesigned course, students think, work hard, like what they are doing, and get good grades that mean something. Faculty also find the course more enjoyable to teach and have more time to devote to other projects.

In addition to engaging students at higher cognitive levels, increasing the effectiveness of student learning, and reviving my own pedagogical methods, designing and teaching a blended course has led to some unexpected benefits. The redesigned course materials and pedagogical approach offer a solid context to introduce graduate teaching fellows to the teaching of literature. Graduate assistants may begin by grading online discussion posts and compositions, then move into using the curriculum materials created during the redesign process to lead some of the small-group discussions and sessions. In effect, the instructor models the best practices of aligning measurable objectives, activities, and assessments, of using technology in meaningful ways, and of increasing student interaction—all while maintaining academic rigor, integrity, and freedom.

This redesigned course is a pedagogically sound scaffold or template that allows a variety (of content and lesson modules) to be continually incorporated. This N-Gen course can accommodate emerging and maturing technology without sacrificing quality, consistency, sustainability, reproducibility, or validity. This combination—of faculty, who can concentrate on explaining course content; teaching fellows, who can work one-on-one with students to improve writing skills; and technology, which can be used in a variety of meaningful ways to meet a variety of learning styles—can work together to improve student learning outcomes.

REFERENCES

Anderson, L. W., Krathwohl, D. R., Airasian, P. W., Cruikshank, K. A., Mayer, R. E., Pintrich, P. R., . . . Wittrock, M. C. (Eds.). (2001). *A taxonomy for learning, teaching, and assessing: A revision of Bloom's taxonomy of educational objectives.* New York, NY: Addison Westley Longman.

Carriveau, R. S. (2010). *Connecting the dots: Developing student learning outcomes and outcome based assessments.* Denton, TX: University of North Texas Center for Learning Enhancement, Assessment, and Redesign.

Krathwohl, D. R. (2002). A revision of Bloom's taxonomy: An overview. *Theory Into Practice, 41*(3), 212–218.

Lawall, S. N. (2002). *Norton anthology of world literature: Beginning to 1650.* (2nd ed.). New York, NY: Norton.

Lombardi, M. M. (2008). *Making the grade: The role of assessment in authentic learning.* Boulder, CO: Educause. Retrieved from http://www.educause.edu/ELI/Making theGradeTheRoleofAssessm/162389

Savory, P., Burnett, A. N., & Goodburn, A. (2007). *Inquiry into the college classroom: A journey toward scholarly teaching.* Bolton, MA: Anker.

Turner, P. M., & Carriveau, R. S. (2010). *Next generation course redesign.* New York, NY: Peter Lang.

University of North Texas. (2011). *Enabling effective teaching: Next generation course redesign.* Retrieved from http://clear.unt.edu/index2.cfm?M = 2000

5

Blended, With a Twist

Robert Hartwell and Elizabeth F. Barkley

A s far as we can tell, our version of blended delivery is rather unusual. We adopted the term in the early 1990s because it seemed the best label for our flexible class structure: Students choose from a menu of online and face-to-face activities in a manner that best meets their personal, scheduling, and learning needs. Although some students choose only activities at the extremes (either all online or all face-to-face), about 60% combine delivery methods, creating an individualized, customized blend that falls somewhere along the continuum. Of the students who combine delivery methods, one student might do 90% face-to-face and 10% online, and another 90% online and 10% face-to-face. Similarly, the four members of the instructional team vary in their teaching responsibilities. One of us interacts with the class only online, another primarily face-to-face, and the remaining two blend both.

The conceptual underpinning of our approach appears closest to *differentiation*, described by Tomlinson and Strickland (2005) as "a systematic approach to planning curriculum and instruction" (p. 6) in which teachers individualize course elements such as content (the stuff we teach), process (the ways learners make meaning of the content), and product (how learners demonstrate what they have come to know, understand, or do). We implemented our version of blended delivery as part of a larger curricular transformation that metamorphosed a struggling music history course into a thriving one. However, before launching into our experiences, we thought it might be useful to offer some background about ourselves, our institution, and our motivations for implementing this kind of delivery.

We are music history instructors at Foothill College, a community college located in the San Francisco Bay area (Los Altos Hills). Founded in 1957, Foothill serves a student population of almost 14,000, 76% of whom attend part-time. Like most California community colleges, students at Foothill are widely diverse in terms of age, ethnicity, and educational background. Based on 2008 institutional research, 48% of our students are traditional college age (24 or younger), while almost 41% are age 30 or older, including 10% who are over 60. Students of European descent represent 39% of the student population, while students of Asian and Hispanic descent represent 29% and 11%. An additional 7% are international students representing 74 different countries. Educational backgrounds also differ widely: 2% of Foothill students do not have a high school diploma, while 36% already hold a college degree, including 10% who hold graduate degrees.

About 15 years ago, we found ourselves in a dispiriting situation: The European-based classical music history course we had been teaching for years was no longer attracting students. As student interest waned, each quarter began with a harrowing question—would our class meet the minimum enrollment requirements to "go" or not? Even when the class was spared cancellation because it reached the minimum enrollment, we found ourselves staring at distressingly disengaged students. Though tempting, we recognized that blaming the students for our course's struggles was counterproductive and wide of the mark. Palmer (1998) speaks eloquently of these moments, noting that in lamenting student indifference to learning, faculty often fail to recognize the connection between this ennui and their passive, mind-numbing instructional methods (p. 42). Necessity, then, was the impetus for our curricular and pedagogical changes.

BLENDED DELIVERY AS A SOLUTION TO THE PROBLEM

Offering students options in terms of face-to-face or online delivery was part of a larger instructional redesign predicated on allowing students considerable choice in pursuing their learning. This move to a student-centered approach involved changes that fell into four broad categories: (a) helping students make connections between their own lives and what we were teaching in the classroom by moving from Western European to multicultural content, (b) presenting students with a flexible menu of learning activities, (c) giving students more direct control over their grades, and (d) encouraging them to create a personalized blend in terms of course delivery. A brief word about the first three is in order before focusing on blended delivery.

Because 61% of Foothill College's student population stems from a variety of non-White ethnicities, our first step in curricular transformation was to change course content from the traditional, European-based focus to a historical survey of the multiple musical genres that have emerged from the American multicultural experience. Titling the course Music of Multicultural

America (MMA), these multicultural curricular inclusions were also consonant with the larger educational landscape. U.S. Department of Education statistics show that minority enrollment in colleges and universities has increased 146% during the period 1984–2004, thereby tripling the number of postsecondary institutions with at least 25% minority enrollment (Lopez, 2006). In light of these and similar statistics, it was difficult to justify music curricula that did not address cultural diversity.

Instead of the structured and sequential learning activities typical of most college curricula, MMA's instructional design offers a menu of learning activities, thus allowing students to make choices that reflect their own interests and learning style. The course is organized into modules (e.g., Native American Music, Jazz, and Urban Folk Revival), with each module containing multiple learning activities. Learners select the modules that interest them and then choose some or all of the activities within the module. The grading structure is designed in such a way that in order to earn sufficient points to pass the course, students must generally complete a minimum of 10 modules. Students are encouraged to work at a level that challenges them, combining activities and topics in ways that best promote their individual learning. Students are also free to determine the order in which they complete the modules. This order may not match the face-to-face schedule, but since the face-to-face sessions are structured as stand alones, one-to-one correspondence between online and face-to-face work is not necessary.

Assessment and evaluation is also student centered. The course is based on a point accrual system. Each learning activity offers a potential number of points correlating to the complexity and challenge of the activity, and students earn points based on the quality of their work. To discourage students from focusing on quantity rather than quality, point penalties equivalent to the maximum possible are imposed for "junk" efforts. It is possible to earn more points than are needed for a good grade, thus allowing students to choose from a menu of available activities until they have achieved the number of points needed for their desired course grade (e.g., 2,000 out of a possible 4,000 plus points are needed to earn an A). Collectively, these choices allow students to complete the course in a manner consistent with their interests, learning preferences, abilities, and schedule.

Flexible course delivery was the fourth component of MMA's curricular transformation. MMA students are encouraged to personalize the course delivery by choosing the learning modality that best suits their needs. Students may work online, attend face-to-face classes, or combine the two in a manner of their choosing.

BENEFITS OF BLENDED DELIVERY

The advent and proliferation of online learning has dramatically changed the educational landscape, creating two institutionally conjoined but notably different avenues for learners in many colleges and universities. From a learning perspective, online and face-to-face learning have their advantages. Speaking broadly, online learning enjoys a flexibility and accessibility that traditional classes do not, and potentially a more interactive, learner-centered environment. Conversely, the structure provided by face-to-face courses can be helpful to students whose self-sufficiency and time management skills are still developing. Achieving a "thoughtful fusion of face-to-face and online learning experiences" (Garrison & Vaughan, 2008, p. 5) by combining these heretofore separate instructional spheres was challenging, but we persevered, drawn by the prospect of creating a flexible learning environment that emphasizes the strengths of each learning modality and encourages students to be "architects of their own learning" (Barkley, 2006, p. 1).

Benefits to Students

We agree with Barr and Tagg's (1995) assertion that colleges and universities often adhere to a *teaching paradigm* rather than a *learning paradigm*, which not only runs counter to most learning research, but confuses the means (teaching) with the end (learning). In Barr and Tagg's learning paradigm, instructors are encouraged to embrace the most effective learning avenues, unencumbered by existing frameworks and institutional inertia. Blended delivery, with its potential benefits to students, was an opportunity to move MMA further in the direction of a learning paradigm.

The manner in which we interpreted and offer blended delivery encourages students to tailor their studies to their lifestyle and learning style. Students who flourish in a lecture format can choose to attend the face-to-face class sessions, while those who prefer to work independently and alone, work online. MMA face-to-face class sessions almost always include a collaborative learning component, which some students dislike. Although we want students to be the primary decision makers in their own learning, we recognize the importance of collaborative learning skills in today's job market and are therefore implementing new collaborative activities outside the face-to-face class structure. For example, a small-group discussion can be conducted in person or in a private discussion forum, after which students write a synthesizing, follow-up essay that they submit as an assignment. We are finding that this option is attractive to many of our online students, particularly our international students.

This degree of choice may also stimulate intrinsic motivation. Research suggests that intrinsic motivation (i.e., choosing an activity for no other purpose than the satisfaction derived from it) is an important component of student success (Brophy, 2004). As Brophy notes, intrinsic motivation tends to occur "under autonomous and self-determined conditions" (p. 13). While these conditions are sometimes difficult to meet in a traditional face-to-face classroom, our blended instructional design, with its concomitant element of student choice, may help foster a sense of autonomy and self-determination. Finally, the flexibility of blended delivery may help students manage multiple demands on their time (e.g., family, work, commuting), which might otherwise cause a student to drop or fail a traditional class. Flexible delivery offers students additional avenues to complete the course successfully.

Benefits to Faculty

California community college instructors live under a veritable 11th Commandment: Thou shalt not teach classes with small enrollments. Because online music classes at Foothill College routinely enjoy more robust enrollments than their traditional counterparts, offering blended courses can potentially protect low-enrollment face-to-face sections from cancellation. For example, a face-to-face section of a course may have only 16 enrollees, but an online section has 56. Because the classes are combined, administrators are more willing to view them as two parts of a single entity (with an average enrollment of 36 students per section). Indeed, several Foothill College faculty members now employ this strategy as a means of protecting low-enrollment face-to-face sections. From the students' perspective, they see face-to-face and online courses in the college class schedule and enroll in one or the other based on their preference. Once the term begins, they learn of their options for blending face-to-face with online, and they then mix up the delivery as they wish.

Blended learning also has the potential to prevent disinterested students from sabotaging class morale. While we hope never to give up on reaching disengaged students, we also acknowledge that some students simply do not want to be in class. The causes of their disengagement are many: parental pressure to be in school, having nothing better to do, or just simple exhaustion as a consequence of work or other life pressures. Whatever the cause, the outcome is the same—their presence has a deleterious effect on class morale; if enthusiasm is contagious, its converse is perhaps even more so. Our approach to blended delivery reframes attendance issues and allows students who are unhappy in the face-to-face environment to work online. Since instituting blended delivery, our classrooms have felt much more energized and engaged.

Finally, just as students have personal preferences for learning in a face-to-face or online classroom environment, so do professors have personal preferences for teaching in either environment. Some of us flourish with the social interaction and the energetic, synchronous, and established meeting times of the traditional classroom, while others prefer the quiet, asynchronous interaction and scheduling flexibility that characterizes the online classroom. Even if we enjoy both environments, a steady dose of either one is less attractive than a blend. Just as teaching exclusively online is not very appealing to any of our team members, we have found it is much easier to create a dynamic face-to-face class session if we only have to do so once or twice a week as opposed to the daily grind of a typical full-time assignment. Along this line, we have also worked out a system that distributes ancillary responsibilities such as course coordination, web page design, grading, forum moderation, and so forth in a way that offers each of our instructional team members a unique blend of activities that take advantage of individual strengths and preferences.

CREATION AND IMPLEMENTATION OF BLENDED DELIVERY

The first challenge was to create an instructional design that could accommodate both modes of course delivery and that used the learning advantages of each modality. A conventional course design, predicated on tests derived from lectures and readings, is not well suited to a course with optional attendance (leaving aside any mention of its learning efficacy). One solution would be to design tests based exclusively on the readings, thus allowing the online and face-to-face students an equal opportunity for success. But then what would be the distinctive function of the face-to-face component? To address this issue, we decided to make the face-to-face class experience a stand-alone learning activity similar to the other activity choices—watching films, attending concerts, visiting historical sites, writing personal reflections, and so forth. Since all students receive their core information from the readings, the face-to-face presentations are one choice in a menu of activities, all designed to expand and deepen student understanding rather than simply revisiting information acquired from the reading.

MMA's Face-to-Face Activities

Because students choose whether they attend face-to-face class sessions, there is a slightly different mix of students in each class. This makes it challenging to foster a sense of classroom community. To address this, we ask the regulars (about 85% of the attending students) to sit close to the front of the classroom, and we encourage them to form groups that will sit and work together throughout the academic term. Class sessions emphasize instructor-guided listening (while new technologies have vastly improved online listening examples, in our opinion there is no substitute for an instructor guiding students through a musical example), performance demonstrations (where we might, for example, play a blues progression on the piano and then show how a blues pianist would vary it in a boogie-woogie or barrelhouse style), and collaborative activities that are designed to be completed within the class session. Single-session collaborative activities prevent the continuity and logistical problems that might otherwise occur because each class meeting attracts a different mix of students. Although these assignments tend to be limited in depth because they are shorter, students can choose to participate in more extensive collaborative activities as one of their part-level assignment choices (see p. 122 on part-level activities).

Students gather their notes, collaborative work products, and individual essay responses to instructor-designed prompts in an in-class portfolio they submit twice during the academic term. Just like every other learning activity, portfolios are evaluated and earn points based on quantity (the number of sessions attended) and quality (thoroughness and thoughtfulness of notes and reflections). Recently we have added a new twist to the portfolio process: peer evaluation. We implemented this change for logistical and pedagogical reasons. Logistically, evaluating the portfolios had become something of a nightmare, producing a veritable mountain of grading. Peer review eases some of that burden and allows us to return the portfolios expeditiously. Pedagogically, students benefit from reviewing course materials as presented in the portfolios of their classmates and from reading the ideas and perspectives of other students.

The peer-review process is carefully structured but with the following basic parameters: (a) Students choose whether to have their portfolios graded by the instructors or to participate in the peer-review process (for which they earn a few extra points), but they are allowed to participate only if they have attended almost all the face-to-face sessions; (b) students evaluate the portfolios in small groups to provide support and a kind of check-and-balance as they do their assessment; (c) we provide a comprehensive assessment rubric as well as guide them on what to look for using presentation slides on a session-by-session basis; and (d) there is an appeals process (complete with a penalty if the appeal is considered a frivolous complaint).

MMA's Online Learning Activities

Online learning activities fall into three categories, with potential point awards reflecting the activity's requisite effort and level of sophistication. First are module-level activities, in which students take open-book multiple-choice quizzes based on the textbook readings. In completing these quizzes, students demonstrate an understanding of basic course information; the quizzes also provide scaffolding for the larger-scale projects. While such things as quizzes fall into the lower levels of cognitive taxonomies, we have retained them because they help ensure coverage of baseline information and provide avenues of success to nonnative English speakers and students with more limited academic skills.

Second are part-level activities (each part consists of about five modules), where students choose to complete midsize projects, such as writing an essay in conjunction with viewing a film, attending a concert or cultural event, visiting a historical site, or participating in a more complex collaborative activity. These larger projects take more time to complete and require students to function within the higher levels of cognitive taxonomies.

Finally, at the comprehensive level, students construct a web-based Musician Portrait or, alternatively, they can design their own project (called Wildcard), which is negotiated with an instructor early in the quarter. For the Musician Portrait, students integrate and synthesize module- and part-level knowledge and understanding by analyzing the musical, ethnic, and historical influences on a musician's work and relating the work to their own lives. They complement their analysis with images, a discography, song lyrics, and URLs of websites for further information. These portraits are retained in a Portrait Gallery, creating a knowledge repository for current and future students.

CHALLENGES IN OUR VERSION OF BLENDED DELIVERY

There have been many challenges offering a course with such extensive flexibility. For example, the course's complexity initially resulted in a lengthy syllabus that was overwhelming to many students, particularly those with limited English or academic skills. It also tended to generate an avalanche of e-mails. While we are here to serve our students, we were spending too much time answering questions. Worse, answering these e-mails demanded still more hours at the computer keyboard (both of us have had repetitive stress problems with our hands). We have implemented several strategies to ameliorate this problem. For example, the course syllabus now begins with two features: Course at a Glance and Quick Start. As their titles imply, these components offer students essential explanations of how the course works so that they can get started on their course work immediately without having to read through too much information.

We have also divided the syllabus into components that are hyperlinked to a main syllabus page, reducing the hard-copy syllabus to a manageable four to five pages. Furthermore, as an inducement to read the syllabus, students can earn points by taking the Syllabus Quiz, an online quiz consisting of multiple-choice questions on how the course works. We are also considering moving toward a graphic syllabus (Nilson, 2007). Finally, we have set aside office hours so students can drop by or phone in if they have questions, scheduled some of the first two weeks' face-to-face time for student orientation, and pushed back our first deadline so students have time to figure things out.

Some students resist a learner-centered approach (Weimer, 2002). More demanding and less familiar than the traditional curriculum, learner-centered teaching places a greater burden of responsibility on students who may or may not have the requisite maturity to participate effectively in new learning strategies. As Felder and Brent (1996) observe, students whose teachers have been telling them everything throughout their primary and secondary educations may not appreciate the sudden removal of this support. Anxiety might also play a role in student resistance—students are sometimes uncomfortable when asked to move outside the predictable educational scenario. Nor should human nature be discounted; students may become resistant when they realize a student-centered approach often requires more work.

RESULTS OF IMPLEMENTING BLENDED DELIVERY

The conception and implementation of this flexible model did not take place overnight. Rather, the curricular transformation from our traditional music history course to MMA was implemented over a five-year period from 1994 to 1999, with subsequent years devoted to refining the instructional design. Collectively, these curricular changes have had an enormous impact on the class. The most obvious barometer of our success is a dramatic rise in enrollment. The traditional music history course had an annual enrollment of 45 students, while MMA grew to an annual enrollment of 1,200 plus within seven years—a dizzying increase of 2,266%.

Because blended delivery was only one of several curricular changes implemented more or less simultaneously, it is difficult to isolate its impact from that of the other changes. However, an anonymous survey conducted five years after the implementation of the curricular transformation offers some indication of student preference for blended delivery. Fifty-eight face-to-face attendees from two different MMA classes were asked to prioritize the four curricular changes (blended delivery, flexible menu of activities, control over their grade, and multicultural content). The results of this survey showed that the majority of students ranked blended delivery as the second or third most important contributor to their success in the course. (Multicultural content and control of grade were ranked highest at priority one.)

We also solicited student comments and feedback in that same survey. Here are some of their anonymous responses:

- "Blended is splendid! I enjoy in-person classes, so I benefit from coming to class. However, I'm not restricted to this and enjoy the freedom to substitute work online at my own pace."
- "I like this idea because there are sometimes [sic] when you just can't attend class because of various reasons. When this happens you tend to fall behind in class (I know this from experience) but having online work can help you not get behind."
- "I love the flexibility. It gives you time to enjoy the class and its contents rather than stress over having to do things you don't like. I hate worksheets, for instance, but I love reading the chapter and taking the quizzes, so it works perfect for me."
- "The flexibility is awesome! It allows the students to plan how she/he wants to approach the class. It is also motivating. It makes the students in complete control."
- "I think the format and structure of this class offers great flexibility. This is a college course, so leaving it up to the student to work for the grade they want in a manner that suits them best creates a level of mutual respect. I wish more of my classes had this option."

The optional class attendance in our version of blended delivery has also offered some unexpected bonuses. We now treat class attendance as a privilege rather than a right, like a driver's license. Since students are awarded points for attending, we feel justified in expecting greater levels of engagement. Disengaged students (e.g., those who are sleeping, text messaging, or not participating in class activities) are encouraged to work online. By week three, we also lock the door once the class starts with the understanding that students not making it to class on time have forfeited their attendance privilege for that day. In a traditional face-to-face class, locking the door or suggesting disengaged students not attend might seem severe, punitive, high schoolish, and pedagogically suspect. In our flexible and blended format, however, late students can go to the college media center and pursue their learning online or just have a cup of coffee, perhaps vowing to leave home a few minutes earlier next time.

REFLECTIONS ON OUR CURRICULAR TRANSFORMATION

Though challenging and still a work in progress, implementing our version of blended learning—along with the other curricular changes—ranks among the best decisions of our teaching careers. Since inaugurating these changes, enrollment is up, student morale is up, and our enthusiasm for teaching is up. The online and face-to-face classes are livelier and populated with more engaged learners. At the conclusion of each quarter, we receive e-mails from multiple students telling us how much they enjoyed the class and how grateful they were for the course's flexibility. From an institutional perspective, these curricular and pedagogical changes have been spectacularly successful. MMA's productivity, a funding calculation based on how many students enter the course and how many students complete it, has skyrocketed, a phenomenon that has elicited enthusiastic support from administrators.

Allowing students to take control—and responsibility—for their learning has been a boon to all concerned. As Weimer (2002) noted, students need to take responsibility for their learning in their quest to become autonomous and self-regulating learners. Almost uniformly, MMA students have welcomed the opportunity to exercise control over their learning. As one student said, "In this class, you stay motivated to learn and work hard because success is up to you." The shared learning responsibility also reframes the instructor-learner dynamic, placing us in a less-authoritarian role. For example, blended delivery defuses the often thorny issues surrounding attendance, thereby enabling us to assume the more rewarding role of learning ally rather than learning adversary.

Perhaps most rewarding is the sense of liberation brought about by these changes. Thanks to MMA's popularity, we are no longer hostages to the vicissitudes of enrollment. The course's new aura of vibrancy and enthusiasm has invigorated our teaching and largely freed us from our earlier Sisyphean struggles with the marginally engaged. Implementing these changes has been a long and complicated process, but we believe the dividends in learning outcomes, student engagement, and renewed job satisfaction have amply rewarded our efforts. As each academic term draws to a close, we acknowledge these benefits and metaphorically raise our glass in celebration of our unusual concoction—blended, with a twist.

REFERENCES

Barkley, E. (2006). Honoring student voices, offering students choices: Empowering students as architects of their own learning. *National Teaching and Learning Forum, 15*(3), 1–6.

Barr, R., & Tagg, J. (1995). From teaching to learning: A new paradigm in undergraduate education. *Change, 27*(6), 12–25.

Brophy, J. (2004). *Motivating students to learn.* Mahwah, NJ: Erlbaum.

Felder, R. M., & Brent, R. (1996). *Navigating the bumpy road to student-centered instruction.* Retrieved from http://www4.ncsu.edu/unity/lockers/users/f/felder/public/Papers/Resist.html

Garrison, D. R., & Vaughan, N. D. (2008). *Blended learning in higher education: Framework, principles, and guidelines.* San Francisco, CA: Jossey-Bass.

Lopez, J. (2006). *The impact of demographic changes on United States Higher Education: 2000–2050.* Chapel Hill: University of North Carolina. Retrieved from http://www.sheeo.org/pubs/demographics-lopez.pdf

Nilson, L. B. (2007). *The graphic syllabus and the outcomes map: Communicating your course.* San Francisco, CA: Jossey-Bass.

Palmer, P. J. (1998). *The courage to teach.* San Francisco, CA: Jossey-Bass.

Tomlinson, C., & Strickland, C. (2005). *Differentiation in practice: A resource book for differentiating curriculum, Grades 9–12.* Alexandria, VA: Association for Supervision and Curriculum Development.

Weimer, M. (2002). *Leaner-centered teaching.* San Francisco, CA: Jossey-Bass.

6

Concluding Thoughts on This Volume

Francine S. Glazer

What continues to impress me about blended learning is its versatility: The instructional design of a course can vary dramatically to reflect the style of the instructor and the nature of the discipline. Common to all successful blended learning courses, though, is active learning in one form or another and, of course, an increased use of technology. The blended learning courses we have seen all incorporate more interactions, among the students and between students and the instructor.

Increased opportunities for interaction engage a larger percentage of the students and help solidify a learning community, an effect that is especially noticeable in large classes. Discussions in class and online incorporate more critical thinking and analysis, and students working collaboratively produce more sophisticated work. The scope of the discussions is broader as students make more connections between what they are learning and their prior knowledge.

Learning objects give students a chance to assess their own understanding and to practice their new skills online before coming to the face-to-face class, and the multimedia appeals to students with different learning styles. Technology can also be used to make online resources easier to access, allowing students to bring more information to bear on their analyses of course content.

We saw examples of front loading—introducing information prior to the in-class activities—and back loading—introducing material in class and using online activities to help the student process that content. Time spent online gives students more time to reflect on and consolidate the content into larger chunks, which in turn enables them to build a more elaborate knowledge framework.

There are a number of questions you should consider as you decide whether you should create a blended learning course. The ideal course is one with high student demand so you can be fairly sure you will teach it again and again. If there are other sections that will continue to be taught face-to-face, you may want to revisit the way student learning outcomes are assessed in those courses as well so that different sections of the course are consistent with each other. In the long run, the institution will benefit—not only will courses be consistent across sections and semesters, but assessment will be more meaningful if the student products are directly comparable.

The extent of institutional support is a critical factor, not only in making the decision to blend or not to blend but also in terms of the type of course you can create. Tracey Gau, for example, is at an institution with instructional designers and multimedia specialists who worked with her as a design team to develop sophisticated learning objects that help students focus on the content. My blended case study, by contrast, was discussion based. As I mentioned in Chapter 2, though, extending the blended activity to the entire course will at some point require me to seek assistance from specialists who can leverage the technology appropriately.

Institutional support also manifests itself in terms of support provided to students. Students may have very different levels of technology access and expertise, and it's essential that the technology not interfere with the learning. Is there an orientation to the learning management system, or are there tutorials online students can access easily?

Finally, consider your own situation. It's wise to know how the institution values this work, especially in terms of tenure and promotion. What other significant time commitments have you taken on? The summer in which you are revising two manuscripts and submitting a grant proposal is probably not the summer to convert a course to a blended format. If you will be an early adopter of this pedagogy at your school, are your colleagues supportive? Will you be challenged about the rigor of your course, or will you be applauded for adopting a student-centered pedagogy?

It is my hope that the examples in this book will spark your imagination as you contemplate your own courses.

Contributors

Alan Aycock is acting director of the Learning Technology Center at the University of Wisconsin–Milwaukee (UWM), where he was the first faculty member to offer a fully online course. Alan presents numerous workshops on blended learning; UWM was one of the first institutions to develop a course redesign program for blended teaching and learning. Prior to joining UWM, Alan was professor of social anthropology and department chair at the University of Lethbridge in Alberta, Canada, where he was named Distinguished Teacher. Despite his full-time appointment at the Learning Technology Center, Alan continues to publish in anthropology and in the scholarship of teaching and learning, and teaches blended and fully online courses.

Elizabeth F. Barkley is an award-winning professor of music at Foothill College in Los Altos Hills, California. With over 30 years' experience as an innovative and reflective teacher, her areas of interest include engaging students through active and collaborative learning, transforming face-to-face and online curricula to meet the needs of diverse learners, the scholarship of teaching and learning, and connecting learning goals with outcomes and assessment. Her major publications in the area of teaching and learning include *Student Engagement Techniques: A Handbook for College Faculty* (San Francisco, CA: Jossey-Bass, 2010) and *Collaborative Learning: A Handbook for College Faculty*, coauthored with K. Patricia Cross and Claire Howell Major (San Francisco, CA: Jossey-Bass, 2004).

Carl Behnke is an assistant professor of hospitality and tourism management at Purdue University, where he teaches courses related to food service operations. Prior to joining the faculty, Carl served as special events chef to the president of Purdue and worked with several companies in locations that include New Orleans, Las Vegas, Chicago, and Switzerland. Carl's research interests include hospitality education and food safety.

129

Tracey M. Gau is a faculty fellow and senior course redesign consultant at the Center for Learning Enhancement, Assessment, and Redesign (CLEAR) at the University of North Texas (UNT). In addition to her work at CLEAR, she has taught for 12 years in the English department at UNT. Her focus is on redesigning core curriculum and large enrollment courses, such as World Literature, Composition, and Shakespeare. Her redesign work has been featured in *Next Generation Course Redesign* (New York, NY: Peter Lang, 2010) and *Transforming the Humanities Classroom for the 21st Century* (Reno, NV: Bent Tree Press, 2009). Tracey received her bachelor's and master's degrees in English from the University of Nebraska at Omaha and her PhD in English from Texas Christian University.

Francine S. Glazer is assistant provost and founding director of the Center for Teaching and Learning at New York Institute of Technology (NYIT). A biologist by training, she also holds a Master Online Teacher certificate from the Illinois Online Network, University of Illinois. Prior to joining NYIT, she was professor of biological sciences and assistant director of the Center for Professional Development at Kean University. She has been working actively with faculty members since 1993. Her current areas of interest include course redesign to incorporate active learning, use of student teams in the classroom, faculty mentoring, and online and blended learning.

Robert Hartwell is a professor of music history at Foothill College. He has published on topics ranging from Renaissance to rock, and most recently has coauthored a series of three books on the history of Western music. Robert also lectures widely within the community, and served as preperformance lecturer for the San Francisco Opera. He is keenly interested in issues of teaching and learning, particularly in connection with the integration of contemporary culture into college curricula. Robert holds a bachelor's degree in piano performance from Sonoma State University, a master's degree in music history from San Francisco State University, and a doctorate in music education from Columbia University.

Index

creating time through, 4–5
in culinary arts, 14–30
danger of, 98
defined, 1
dialogic effect of, 65
and disinterested students, 119–120
and face-to-face time, 7–8
institutional support for, 128
methods of, 3, 4
and online tests, 21–22
and organized knowledge, 8
pitfalls unique to, 5
reasons for using, 28
and self-directed learning, 8–11
and student expectations, 41–42
student participation in, 6–7
and time management, 40–42
unique feature of, 1
versatility of, 127
blended learning courses
in anthropology, 59–80
in culinary arts, 13–30
description of, 1
development of, 21
in genetics, 31–43
layering of, 5–6
in literature, 87–113
in music history, 116–126
preference for teaching, 83
Bloom, B. S. E., 15
Body Ritual Among the Nacirema, 69
Boehrer, J., 32
Brent, R., 123
Bridges, M. W., 3
Burnett, A. N., 105

Carriveau, Ronald S., 100
case study
as a blended activity, 34–35
complications, 46–47
discussion questions, 46, 47
genetics course, 32–33
introduction of characters in, 45–46
mediation, 47–50
role play, 35–36

stages of, 33–34
student reactions to, 36–37
timeline issues, 37–38
Chatfield, K., 5, 6
Chen, C., 17
Chickering, A. W., 35
Christian, W., 4
class attendance, 72, 124
classroom assessment techniques (CATs)
description of, 72
for face-to-face component, 71
subtypes of, 72–75
classroom debriefings, 10, 35, 62
classroom discussions, 73, 96
clickers
advantages of, 75–76
description of, 75
for feedback, 76
implications of, 77
think-pair-share technique for, 76
collaborative learning, 96, 98, 118
collaborative work, 4, 121
community garden, 33, 45, 47
Confucian enlightenment, 92
constructed response items
evaluation of, 107–108
purpose of, 103
summative assessment, 105–106
constructivism philosophy, 19
contract learning, 9
Cottell, P. G., Jr., 4, 32
course design/redesign
anthropology course, 60, 78–80, 82
by faculty, 3, 4, 5
literature course, 88–91
music history course, 116–117
objective of, 89
types of interactions in, 2
course management system
anthropology course, 61, 67, 78, 81, 82
culinary arts, 24
genetics course, 34, 41
course materials
anthropology course, 67, 73, 78, 80